Bull's Eye- A stock market investment guide for beginners

Sharma Raj Kumar

Published by Sharma Raj Kumar, 2022.

BULL'S EYE- A STOCK MARKET INVESTMENT GUIDE FOR BEGINNERS

First edition. March 21, 2022.

ISBN: 979-8215193297

Written by Sharma Raj Kumar.

Table of Contents

Capital Market

A market in which buyers and sellers engage in the trade of financial securities such as bonds, stocks, etc. Both individuals and institutions can be participants in this market.

In other words, a Capital market is a place where those having surplus funds lend/invest to/with those who need funds by way of purchase and sale of securities.

The user of funds gets funds by the sale of securities i.e., equity or bond, and the supplier of funds gets invested in the securities for future returns.

The suppliers of funds in the capital market could be; individuals, corporates, pension funds, mutual funds, insurance companies, charitable trusts, etc. while the users of funds could be; the government, corporates, individuals, etc.

The capital market consists of the Primary market & Secondary Market. We will understand the difference between primary & secondary markets in detail subsequently.

Capital markets can further be classified based on the type of security. It could be the stock market- Where equity shares of a company trade. Bond Market- Were debt securities i.e., bonds, debentures trades.

Most of the primary & secondary markets are now digital marketplaces like Bombay Stock Exchange, New York Stock Exchange, etc.

Capital Market Vs Financial Market

Capital Market is where companies & government raises capital by selling debt (bonds) or equity instruments. Capital market is also known as financial market used by companies to raise long-term funds by the sale of long-term bonds and where equity-backed securities are bought or sold.

Financial Market is a broader term that includes all types of markets used to raise funds by exchanging securities, assets & contracts. Some of the prominent financial markets are the money market, stock market, bond market, forex market, commodity market & real estate market.

So, the capital market is a component of the financial market on which the long-term trading of equity shares and bonds takes place.

Components of equity market

- New Issue Market or Primary Market
- Secondary Market
- Financial Institutions & intermediaries

Primary Market

A market where the securities are sold first time by the issuer. For example; A company needs to raise funds by way of the sale of shares. To do this it will issue an Initial public offering (IPO) through which the company calls for investors to purchase shares and participate in the future growth prospects of the company. The sale proceeds of the share will be utilized by the company for various purposes, it could be capital expansion, de-leveraging from existing debt, etc.

The investor will invest in the IPO if he found;

1. the prospects of future growth of the company to be lucrative and
2. the shares to be issued are at discount to the fair market value.

Initial discount enables the investor to book **listing gains** i.e., the difference between allotment price and the share listing price.

When the share gets listed in the market and the public is allowed to trade in that at this point of time many short-term investors exit the position by booking listing gains. But long-term investors having a vision and understanding of the company's model continue to participate in the company's growth by holding the share for further appreciation. They are rewarded by good companies by way of appreciation in the share price/dividend earned.

The dividend is the sharing of net profit of the company amongst the shareholders in the ratio of their shareholdings.

Though not compulsory but good companies take care of their shareholders by sharing profits by way of dividends. Companies can retain the profit for future capital expansion or some other purpose and it will reflect in the increase in net worth of the company.

Both the new companies (through IPO) & existing companies (through FPO) can issue securities and raise funds.

The companies that issue their shares are called issuers and the process of issuing shares to the public is known as a public issue.

This entire process involves various intermediaries like Merchant Banker, Bankers to the Issue, Underwriters, Registrars to the Issue, etc. All these intermediaries are registered with regulators and are required to abide by the prescribed norms to protect the investor.

The Primary Market is, hence, the market that provides a channel for the issuance of new securities by issuers to raise capital. The securities may be issued at face value, or a discount/premium in various forms such as equity, debt, etc. They may be issued in the domestic and/or international markets.

Features of primary markets include:

1. The securities are issued by the company directly to the investors.

1. The company receives the money and issues new securities to the investors.

1. The primary markets are used by companies to set up new ventures/businesses or for expanding or modernizing the existing business

1. Primary market performs the crucial function of facilitating capital formation in the economy.

Process Flow in Primary Market

A company willing to raise capital from the public is required to prepare an offer document giving sufficient information and disclosures, which enables potential investors to make an informed decision.

Accordingly, the offer document is required to contain details about the company, its promoters, the project, financial details, purpose of raising the money, terms of the issue, etc.

The issuer company engages a merchant banker registered with the concerned regulator (in India SEBI) to prepare the offer document. Besides, due diligence in preparing the offer document, the merchant banker is also responsible for ensuring legal compliance. The merchant banker facilitates the issue in reaching the prospective investors (marketing the issue).

The draft offer document thus prepared is filed with the regulator and is made available for public viewing.

The regulator reviews the draft offer document and may issue observations on the draft offer document to ensure that adequate disclosures are made by the issuer company/merchant bankers in the offer document to enable the investor to make an informed investment decision on the issue.

The regulator's observations on the draft offer document are forwarded to the merchant banker, who incorporates the necessary changes and files the final offer document with the regulator, Registrar of Companies (ROC), and stock exchange(s). This is made available on websites of the merchant banker, stock exchange(s), and regulator.

Opening of the Issue

After completing legal formalities, the issuer company issues advertisements in newspapers and the issue is open to the public for subscription.

If the prospective investor is interested in subscribing to the shares of the issuer company based on what is disclosed in the offer document, he can apply for its shares (or debentures) before the issue closes, by duly filling up the application form and making the payment.

The entire back-office operation of the public issue, including the processing of application forms, the despatch of refunds, allotment of securities, are handled by the Registrar to the Issue (RTI) on behalf of the issuer company.

Allotment and Listing

The issue then closes (investors cannot apply beyond the closing date) and the shares are allotted to the applicants proportionally or on a lottery basis if there is an over subscription.

The merchant banker and RTI finalize the 'basis of allotment'. This is approved by the stock exchange officials and the basis of allotment is made available on the website of RTI.

Upon allotment, investors will receive shares in their Demat account. The amount received from investors who could not get shares allotted will be refunded back within the regulator's prescribed timelines.

The shares of the company will now get listed on the stock exchange (Secondary Market) on a predetermined date and will be available for trading.

Listing of Securities

On the listing of securities, the shares and debentures are officially started quoting on the trading floor of the stock exchange. These listings will take place only for the shares or debentures which fulfill certain pre-specified criteria fixed by the regulator/exchange.

Objective of Listing

- It enables supervision and control of dealing in securities.
- With the supervision and control the interest of shareholders and investors is protected.
- It avoids the concentration of economic power in a few hands. Anyone with a trading and Demat account can buy or sell securities.
- It ensures liquidity and transparency on the liquidity position of security.

Secondary Market

A market where the securities are traded after initial listing. So, in the secondary market only existing or previously issued securities trades unlike in the primary market where the fresh securities are issued for the first time.

When we refer to the term stock market, it generally means secondary market. Stock exchanges like the Bombay Stock Exchange or New York Stock Exchange, etc., provide an organized way of trading in secondary market securities.

Every country has its exchanges where companies list their securities for trading. The biggest stock exchange in the world in terms of market capitalization is the New York Stock Exchange.

The market capitalization of a stock exchange is the multiplication of the number of outstanding shares of the companies listed on the exchange x the present market value of the share.

The need for a stock exchange arises from the need of an investor in securities to liquidate the position with ease and the need for a new buyer to invest in the securities with ease. The stock exchange provides liquidity and ensures the security of the transaction.

Activities of stock exchanges are regulated by a regulatory body to maintain transparency and high ethical standards with prudent risk management. The transactions on stock exchanges take place within the regulatory mandates issued by the regulatory body. It is to protect the interest of the investors.

In stock exchanges, both genuine investors and speculators can participate.

Investment Vs Speculation

Traders in securities can be broadly classified into three categories; Investor, Speculator & Arbitrager. In any market, these three types of traders can be found easily.

Investor

An investor is someone who has purchased security with the intention to

- hold it for a longer period and to gain from the price appreciation of the security on account of improvement in the fundamentals of the company
- earning on account of dividends distributed by the company from the profits earned to the equity shareholders.

The key differentiator is the tenor & the intent of the purchaser of the share. Generally, an Investor will invest in a stock after doing some kind of fundamental analysis of the company and on getting satisfied that the investment is likely to give a positive return over a period of time.

Speculator

A speculator purchases or sells securities to get benefited quickly from the favourable movement of the stock without being fundamentally confident of the stock's growth potential. Speculators generally take a position for a day or two.

Both investment and speculation are open to risk but the degree of risk varies. Speculation will be subject to higher risk, as against this investment will be for a more stable return.

Investment is something that you have done after a thorough analysis of the instrument/company in which you are going to invest thus ensuring the safety of the principal with decent returns.

Another key point of difference in investment and speculation will be the instrument itself. Investors generally invest by purchasing stock and holding it as against this a speculator can deal in options, futures where he is leveraging heavily.

The speculator can also sell the stock without holding it with the intention to square off the position before the day end or expiry of the option / future derivative series.

We will discuss options and futures in detail in subsequent chapters.

The asset class that can be treated as investment includes stocks, mutual funds, bonds, physical commodities like gold, debentures, real estate, etc.

The assets that are generally treated as speculative are options, futures, cryptocurrency, junk bonds, etc.

The speculators can further be classified into four categories

Bull, Bear, Stag & Lame duck

Bull

Speculators who are always bullish on the stock. I.e., They mostly take positions in anticipation of the stock going up are called Bulls. With this expectation a Bull purchases stock to sell it at a higher price.

Bear

Speculators who expect the stock to go down i.e., price reduction. He sells the stock to buy it back at a lower price. Many a time a Bear speculator sells the stock without physically holding it with the intention to square off the position quickly, this is known as naked selling.

Stage

Stag is a cautious speculator who buys shares through an IPO with the intent to sell at a premium with listing gains. He generally buys shares of companies that are in heavy demand and where the likelihood of listing gains is higher.

Lame-duck

A bearish trader who has sold the stock with the intent to buy it back when the prices fall but is not able to do so as the prices instead of falling have increased and now the trader does not have money to square-off his position is known as the lame duck. In such scenarios, the lame-duck trader has to default or go bankrupt.

Arbitrager

An arbitrager trades in the market to get benefited from the price differential existing between two different markets.

Example: A share of Bajaj Auto is trading on both NSE & BSE and the price on NSE is 3513.90/95 & on BSE it is 3515.15/20. In such a scenario a trader having access to both NSE and BSE terminals will quickly buy shares of Bajaj Auto from NSE @ 3513.95 & sell the same number of shares on BSE @3515.15.

This buying on one exchange and selling on another generally happens at the same time to avoid change in prices. In this process, the trader has secured a profit of Rs1.20 per share. The net gain/ loss will be arrived at after deducting the brokerage & taxes applicable on this trade.

Investment as defined earlier is a calculated call to put your money in an asset after a thorough analysis of growth potential, the safety of principal, and adequacy of returns. So, for an activity to be called an investment it should fulfill the following criteria

- Analysis of company: Understanding the business, soundness of financials & its growth potential.
- Buying at a bargain price to reduce chances of incurring serious losses.
- The return potential should be adequate to take the risk, otherwise, put your money in risk-free returns like Govt Securities or Bank deposits.

Understanding the business is very important because the stock prices go up only if the prospects of the business are good.

Speculation on the other hand is betting on the stock without completing your homework and anticipating high returns without being backed by any fundamental analysis.

Speculation though generally classified as trading with a short-term view but I believe, if you have bought any stock for whatsoever time horizon & if you have not done its fundamental analysis then it's just a matter of chance that you can end up earning some money and its as good as short-term speculation.

If you wish to trade with both speculative as well as investment objectives then you should keep both at arms' distance and should set clear guidelines on the criteria of such trade. Further adhering to your guidelines is a must. It is advisable to keep the stop loss on every trade to avoid big losses. Further, keep the portion of the speculative portfolio to a max of 10% of your total portfolio.

The performance of the stock market depends on three important factors

1. Real Growth of companies listed on the stock market i.e., increase in earnings.
2. Speculative growth or fall fuelled by the overall sentiments of the investors.
3. Moderate Inflation results in a general increase in prices and thus an increase in companies' performance fuelling growth. But inflation if goes beyond control will ultimately increase the cost for the company and thus the stock market will react negatively.

Financial Institution & Intermediaries

S tock Broker: Only stockbrokers registered with the stock exchange can provide the services of stockbroking & can execute the trade on behalf of their clients

Stock exchanges are required to provide licenses to the stockbrokers to undertake broking business through its platform.

An investor has to execute a trade through a stockbroker. A stockbroker provides the following services

1. Electronic trading platform.
2. Facility for placing orders through an electronic platform, telephone.
3. Issuing contract notes for transactions undertaken through them by their clients.
4. Ensuring financial soundness of its clients by recovering margins / full amount before allowing them to execute a trade and also for the subsequent mark to market position.
5. Obtain KYC of the clients for ensuring genuineness.
6. Circulating changes in guidelines related to security trading to keep clients updated.

Depository

The depository is the electronic register of shares. It provides the facility of holding and transecting of shares/securities in electronic form. When an investor purchases some shares, the shares are transferred from the seller's depository account to the buyer's depository account. Earlier the companies have to transfer shares physically & it takes a lot of time along with the risk of misplacing / duplicity of securities. To overcome these problems the depository concept has come into existence. The share certificates are converted into digital forms and are credited to the clients' Demat account. In India NSDL & CDSL are providing depository services.

The benefit of Depository in Primary Markets

When a company issues its shares through the IPO process, it has to allot shares to the investor. In the absence of an electronic depository, the company will have to allot shares in physical form, it will need printing of a large number of certificates. This process involves the risk of loss in transit, fake / forged certificates and also consumes lots of time. Depository services reduce these risks and time in a significant manner by issuing shares in electronic form i.e., as a simple accounting entry.

The benefit of Depository in Secondary Markets

The electronic depository will eliminate the use of large volumes of paper certificates and thus reduce the wastage of paper, reduce the time involved in settlement cycles, reduce chances of fraud, and delay in transfer of ownership. For the government, it eliminates chances of tax evasion by way of charging & recovering stamp duty digitally.

Bank

As the purchase and sale of shares involves money so the bank's role will certainly come into the picture. When an investor purchases shares, their account gets debited and the amount is transferred to the broker. Brokers in turn will settle the trade with clearing members and exchange. Further banks as an institution invest their surplus amount in securities/equities with the intent to earn higher returns, within the overall limits prescribed by regulators for such activities.

Clearing Corporation

It provides clearing and settlement services for trades in securities. Clearing houses play a crucial role in interbank transaction settlement and in a similar way clearing corporations help in the settlement of securities between buyers and sellers. A clearing house acts as a middle man on behalf of both the seller and the buyers and takes the opposite position of each side of a trade. Clearing house improves the efficiency of the markets and adds stability to the financial system.

Types of Securities
Equity

Equity is the capital owned by the owner of a company. The book value of equity can be arrived at as a difference between assets and liabilities. The portion of assets which is not funded by the bank and outside liabilities is known as the owner's contribution or commonly known as equity.

Book Value: The value of owner's capital invested in the company as per the balance sheet i.e., Asset- Liabilities.

Assets: Current Assets + Non-Current Assets

Liabilities: Current + Non-Current Liabilities

Current Assets: Any asset in the balance sheet which can be converted to cash within the operating cycle or a maximum of one year is known as a current asset. Example: Cash, Inventory, Receivables.

Non-Current Assets: It includes Fixed Assets (e.g., Plant & machinery) + Other non-current & intangible assets like goodwill & intellectual property rights.

Current Liabilities: Liabilities payable within the operating cycle or a maximum of one year are termed as current liabilities. Example: Short term debt payable within one year, working capital debt, trade payables (within one year), part of long-term debt payable in next one year.

Non-Current Liabilities: It includes long-term loans payable beyond one year. Any other fixed financial commitments.

Market Value: The present value of share price in the secondary market can be different than the value evident in the balance sheet. The value of the owner's capital invested in the company is determined by the market value of its shares i.e., a total number of outstanding shares X share price in the market.

In this book, equity will be referred to as the market value of equity. The market value of equity can be lower or higher than the book value. The market prices of shares indicate the future market value of the company as against this book value of shares indicates, the past financial value of the company as on the date of balance sheet.

An investor in the equity share of a company becomes a fractional owner of the company. It gives the owner of the equity shareholder a right to vote in the annual general meeting thus he gets a say in the working of the company. The equity shareholder is entitled to receive dividends from the profit made by the company. But the final decision on the rate of dividend and the pay-out is the company's discretion.

Companies are not bound to declare dividends every year. They can keep the potion of profit for subsequent growth of the company. Dividend pay-out also depends upon the availability of surplus funds and thus if a company is not making enough profit, it can avoid paying dividends.

The common equity shareholders get dividends only from the profit left after paying for interest, tax, debentures & preference dividends.

The equity shares are the permanent liability of a company and are paid only when the company winds up its business. These shares are freely transferable enabling trading on the equity shares through stock exchanges.

The equity shareholder has the last right on the assets of the company after payment of all other dues thus making it the riskiest asset class. With high risk, equity shares also have the potential to generate high returns.

45

Commodity

Commodities like sugar, tea, steel, oil, etc., are also traded on exchanges as their prices also keep on changing with changes in demand and supply matrix. To provide an orderly evolution of price commodity exchanges have come into existence.

These exchanges are used by commodity traders to hedge their exposure against adverse movement of the prices. In India, MCX is the biggest commodity exchange. The trading on commodity exchanges takes place using derivative instruments like futures and options. We will be discussing the future and options in detail in subsequent chapters.

The commodity hedging takes place by taking a position in the derivatives market which is opposite to the position in the cash market thus reducing the effect of risk associated with a change in the price.

Hedging: Use of financial derivative instruments to protect against the adverse moment in the underlying asset. (Will discuss in detail in subsequent chapters)

Currency

Every country has its currency. For concluding trade there is a need to exchange one country's currency with another country's currency. This basic need of conversion of currency for settlement of trades is fulfilled by the use of Banking Channels which buy one currency and sell another currency against it.

The currency market is one of the biggest markets in the world spread across the entire globe, more commonly known as the international currency market.

Participants in this market include banks, corporations, central banks, hedge funds, retail forex brokers, investors, speculators, investment firms, etc. It facilitates global transactions including loans, trade settlements, investments, overseas corporate acquisitions.

It is not a single market but an interlinked chain of global computer networks of large banks and brokerage firms through which the trades in currency take place. It is the largest financial market in the world with an average daily trading volume of $5 trillion.

This movement of currency will have an implication on the movement of share prices. Thus, for any stock trader, knowing the currency market/commodity market / fixed income securities market is a must.

Fixed Income Securities Bonds

Also known as fixed-income securities, bonds are debt instruments issued by companies to raise funds from the market. A Bond is a loan given by the buyer to the issuer of the instrument, in return for interest.

Bonds can be issued by companies, financial institutions, and also Government. Apart from the interest income, the bondholder will receive its principal back on maturity (except in the case of perpetual bonds with no maturity date).

Bonds are normally considered conservative investments in comparison to stocks and in case the issuer goes bankrupt then bonds will generally be having a senior charge in comparison to the common equity which is most risky.

Bond prices vary inversely to the interest rate the reason can be that investors would like to lock their investment in higher coupon-paying bonds when the general interest rates are falling resulting in increased demand for the bond which in turn will result in bond prices going up in the falling interest rate scenario. Similarly, when the market interest rates are going up the bond investors will try to exit from low-interest-paying bonds to move their investment in higher interest-paying instruments resulting in a decrease in demand for the bond and thus a fall in bond price.

Government bonds are assumed to be the safest as it is backed by a guarantee of sovereign and thus chances of default are extremely low. In comparison to Government bonds, the bonds issued by corporates for raising funds carry risk and this risk varies as per the financial position of the company which is assessed by various credit rating agencies. Thus, the interest on corporate bonds will certainly be higher than the interest paid on government bonds.

The interest or the coupon payment is directly linked to the risk involved and as corporate bonds are assumed to be riskier than government bonds thus, they attract higher interest payment obligations.

Terms associated with Bonds

Bills

Debt securities were issued for less than one year. In the US it is 52 weeks

Notes

Debt securities issued for a maturity period of one year - ten years

Bonds

Debt securities issued for maturity beyond 10 years. Generally, up to 30 years with semi-annual /annual coupon payments.

Coupon Rate

A coupon is the interest payment that the bond issuer will pay to the bondholder at a given frequency (generally semi-annually).

Fixed-rate bonds

Fixed-rate bonds are issued with a fixed interest rate for the entire tenor of the bond. The interest rate does not change with changing market conditions and gives a stable return.

Floating rate bonds

In the case of floating rate bonds, the interest will generally be linked to a certain floating rate benchmark and the interest keeps on changing with the change in the benchmark rate (Ex: Libor/ Federal Fund rate / RBI Repo / Inflation, etc.) during the tenor of the bond. The interest gets reset at a given periodic interval depending upon the change in the underlying benchmark rate. The yield on floating rate bonds keeps on changing and realigning it with the changing interest rate scenario.

Floating rate bonds are good in the scenario when interest rates are going up. In this case, the coupon will also go up and thus the bondholder will not lose in comparison to the fixed-rate bonds in which the bondholder is not able to participate in the market. As against this in case of a falling interest rate scenario, the floating rate bondholder will be at disadvantage to the fixed interest rate bondholder.

So floating rate bonds are good investments when the interest rates have already fallen significantly and are expected to go up whereas fixed-rate bonds are good investments when the interest rates have peaked and are now looking to go down thus fetching a higher return in comparison to the prevailing market rate.

Zero-Coupon Bonds

Zero-coupon bonds are issued at a deep discount to the face value and the issuer will not pay any interest during the tenor of the bond. On maturity, the face value of the bond will be paid.

The interest income to the bondholder is compensated by the deep discount on the issuing price in comparison to the face value.

Inflation-Linked Bonds

The interest rate on inflation-linked bonds will be linked to CPI (Consumer price index) or WPI (Wholesale price index) of the issuer /targeted country to take care of the rising inflation. The interest offered on such bonds will be lower in comparison to the normal fixed interest bonds as there is an opportunity for the bondholder to fetch a higher return in case the inflation goes up.

In the US, TIPS (Treasury inflation-protected securities) are issued for the maturity of 5,10-30 years.

Perpetual Bonds

Perpetual bonds are issued with no maturity date. The issuer of the bond will keep on paying coupon interest at the agreed rate till the existence of issuing company or recalling of the bonds. The issuer of the bond is under no obligation to pay back the principal though the issuer is under obligation to keep paying the coupon interest at the prescribed frequency. In this scenario, the credit risk becomes very high as the principal repayment is under question.

In the case of perpetual bonds, the time of redemption is at the discretion of the issuer so he may or may not redeem the issue. In such scenarios, this type of bond is favourable to the issuer as they are under no specific timelines obligation to repay the debt raised by floating these bonds. The issuer when found comfortable can redeem these bonds by paying back the amount to the bondholders.

Generally, perpetual bonds pay a higher interest rate in comparison to the normal fixed interest rate bonds with prescribed maturity. The reason is a higher risk of principal payment.

Convertible Bonds

Bonds that can be converted to common equity shares either at any point in time or on a given maturity date are called convertible bonds.

The conversion ratio (bond to equity) and conversion date will be predetermined. During the tenor of the bond, the bond will be like any other normal bond and will continue to pay interest. The conversion ratio decides the number of shares the bondholder will receive by surrendering one bond. The conversion price is the price of the common equity share at which the bond is converted to shares.

Corporate Bonds

Bonds issued by private and public sector corporations to raise money from the market. The corporate issuing bond will pay the agreed coupon interest to the subscribers and on maturity will pay back the principal amount. The pricing of corporate bonds depends upon the credit rating and the perceived credit risk involved of the issuing corporate.

Municipal Bonds

Bonds are issued by the state, cities, and other local government bodies like municipal corporations. These bonds are issued to raise funds, run the municipal body, and execute public utility projects. Generally, these bonds offer tax benefits to the subscribers. Municipal bonds are of three types

Revenue Bonds

The repayment of these bonds is backed by the revenue generated from a specific project for which the amount is raised such as highway tolls, etc. These are generally non-recourse bonds, meaning if the revenue source dries up the buyer will not have recourse to other sources of income of the municipal body.

General Obligation Bonds

These bonds are paid from the tax collected by the municipal body and are not secured by any assets.

Conduit Bonds

Municipal bodies issue bonds to raise money for public utility offices like colleges, hospitals, etc, and these colleges, hospitals on behalf of which the municipal body has raised money are called conduit borrowers. The conduit borrower repays the amount to the issuer who in turn pays the interest and principal on the bonds to the bondholders.

Investment-grade bonds

Bonds with high credit ratings indicate low default risk, in comparison to other high-yield bonds. Generally, the yield of investment-grade bonds will be lower than that of bonds with higher credit risks. The bonds with credit ratings of Baa (by Moody's) or BBB (by Fitch & S&P) and above are generally treated as investment-grade bonds.

High Yield Bonds / Junk Bonds

Bonds with a low credit rating indicating a high risk of default are termed as High Yield Bonds as the issuer has to offer a higher interest rate or higher discount on the face value of these bonds in comparison to investment-grade bonds. The yields will be higher as the chances of default are higher.

Risks associated with bonds

credit risk

The risk is that the company will default in timely payment of interest or principal payment.

Interest rate risk

The price of bonds will go down in case the market interest rates are rising. Generally, in the case of high-yield bonds, the fall in the price of bonds will be much more than the investment-grade bonds. As the risk is high, the investor will try to quickly liquidate the position in the rising interest rate scenario and thus resulting in a greater fall in the price.

Another factor is that bonds with longer tenors will have higher interest rate risk than bonds with shorter maturities (assuming both are having similar credit qualities) as the bonds with a longer maturity will have more time for an interest rate change.

Economic Risk

When the economy of a country is under stress the investors will try to move away from their investment in the high yield bonds as they will shift their investment to quality assets where their principal will be relatively safe. In such scenarios earning high on the principal is not the focus. The focus will be on the safety of the principal. Thus, the funds will flow towards government bonds (US Treasury bonds) as the government is assumed not to default in payments. In such scenarios, the fall in the price of high-yield bonds will be significant in comparison to other investment-grade bonds.

These situations can result in credit risk as a company that is already facing problems due to economic downturn might not be able to generate enough revenue to meet the interest and principal repayment obligations on the bonds as well as they will not be able to raise fresh funds from the market at competitive rates as the market will compare fresh issue prices with the existing issue of the company and will demand higher discount/coupon for increased risk.

Liquidity risk

Liquidity risk is the risk that investors are not able to sell their bonds at the true value of the bond because of low volumes. Bonds are open to liquidity risk depending upon their investment grade. A high yield bond will be less liquid as volumes will be low and thus liquidity risk will be higher in the case of high yielding bonds in comparison to the low yield of investment-grade bonds.

Call risk

In case a bond is having a call option then the issuer of the bond can call back the bonds at any point of time before the maturity. Generally, the issuer will do so when the interest rates are falling and bond prices are going up. The intention behind this will be to replace higher interest-paying bonds with lower interest-paying bonds as the interest rates are falling and fresh securities will be issued with much lower interest payment obligations. It deprives the bondholder of earning a higher interest rate on their investment when the interest rates are falling.

Yield

The yield of a bond is the annualized return the bond is going to give to its investor. The relationship between yield and bond price is inverse i.e., the higher the price of bond the lower will be the yield, and vice-versa.

Current Yield

Let's assume you have bought a bond with a face value of $10000 and it is currently paying you $550 p.a. than the current yield on the bond will be

(Annual interest X100) / Price

In the above case, the current yield will be 5.5%

In case the investor has bought a bond at a premium or discount the current yield is going to adjust accordingly. Example: You have bought a bond having a face value of $10000 @ $9950 and the bond is paying an annual coupon of $550 then the current yield for this bond will be ($550X100/$9950) =5.527% instead of 5.5%.

In another case you bought a bond having a face value of $10000 from the secondary market @10050 and the fixed annual coupon is $550 then the current yield on this bond will be ($550X100/$10050) = 5.472% instead of 5.5%

Yield to Maturity

Yield to maturity is the amount of return generated by a bond in case the bondholder keeps it till maturity. It considers the compound interest by assuming that the coupon received will be reinvested to increase the return.

After this basic introduction of the Primary & Secondary market, we will focus on the Equity segment for the remaining part of the book. We will use the national stock exchange of India to illustrate the concepts.

Index and portfolio creation

The index measures the performance of a basket of securities using standardized metrics & methodology. In India NSE indices limited (formerly known as India Index Services & Product Limited), or NSE Indices, owns and manages a portfolio of 67 indices under the NIFTY branch. Knowing these indices is very useful in passive investment. By simply following the stocks tracked by these indices an investor can form a portfolio with risk and return similar to the indices.

NSE Indices publishes indices in the following segments

Broad Market Indices: NIFTY 50, NIFTY Next 50, NIFTY 100, NIFTY 200, NIFTY 500 NIFTY Midcap 150, NIFTY Midcap 50, NIFTY Midcap 100, NIFTY Small cap 250, NIFTY Small cap 50, NIFTY Small cap 100, NIFTY Mid-Small cap 400.

Sectoral Indices: NIFTY Auto, NIFTY Bank, NIFTY Financial Services, NIFTY FMCG, NIFTY IT, NIFTY Media, NIFTY Metal, NIFTY Pharma, NIFTY Private Bank, NIFTY PSU Bank, NIFTY Realty

Thematic Indices: NIFTY Aditya Birla Group, NIFTY Commodities, NIFTY CPSE, NIFTY Energy, NIFTY India Consumption, NIFTY Infrastructure, NIFTY Mahindra Group, NIFTY MNC, NIFTY PSE, NIFTY PSE, NIFTY Service Sector, NIFTY Tata Group, NIFTY Tata Group 25% Cap, NIFTY 100 Liquid 15, NIFTY Midcap Liquid 15, NIFTY 50 Shariah, NIFTY Shariah 25, NIFTY 500 Shariah

Strategy Indices: NIFTY 100 Equal Weight, NIFTY 100 Low Volatility 30, NIFTY 50 Arbitrage, NIFTY 50 Futures, NIFTY 50 Futures

TR, NIFTY Alpha 50, NIFTY Dividend Opportunities 50, NIFTY High Beta 50, NIFTY Low Volatility 50, NIFTY 50 Dividend Points, NIFTY 100 Quality 30, NIFTY 50 Value 20, NIFTY Growth Sector 15, NIFTY 50 PR 1 X Inverse, NIFTY 50 PR 2 x Leverage, NIFTY 50 TR 2x Leverage, NIFTY 50 TR 1 X Inverse

We will discuss in brief some of the key indices.

Nifty 50

The NIFTY 50 is the flagship index on the National Stock Exchange of India Ltd. (NSE). The Index tracks the behaviour of a portfolio of blue-chip companies, the largest and most liquid Indian securities. It includes 50 of the approximately 1600 companies listed on the NSE, captures approximately 65% of its float-adjusted market capitalization, and is a true reflection of the Indian stock market.

The NIFTY 50 covers major sectors of the Indian economy and offers investment managers exposure to the Indian market in one efficient portfolio. The Index has been trading since April 1996 and is well suited for benchmarking fund's portfolio, launching index funds, and index-based derivatives.

A company that comes out with an IPO will be eligible for inclusion in the index if it fulfills the normal eligibility criteria for the index like impact cost, market capitalization, and floating stock.

The constituents should be available for trading in the derivatives segment (Stock Futures & Options market) on NSE.

Replacement of Stock from the Index: A stock may be replaced from an index for the following reasons:

Compulsory changes like corporate actions, delisting, etc. In such a scenario, the stock having the largest free-float market capitalization and satisfying other requirements related to liquidity, turnover, and free float will be considered for inclusion.

When a better candidate is available in the replacement pool, which can replace the index stock i.e., the stock with the highest free-float market capitalization in the replacement pool has at least twice the free-float market capitalization of the index stock with the lowest free-float market capitalization. (Source: NSE)

You can access the details of the above index by visiting the NSE website **https://www1.nseindia.com/supra_global/content/iisl/iisl_fact_sheets.htm**

The performance of the stock market/index depends on three important factors

- Real Growth of companies listed on the stock market i.e., increase in earnings.

- Speculative growth or fall fuelled by the overall sentiments of the investors.

- Moderate Inflation results in a general increase in prices and thus an increase in companies' performance fuelling growth. But inflation if goes beyond control will ultimately increase the cost for the company and thus the stock market will react negatively.

Portfolio Creation using Index

Tracking this index and creating a portfolio that is a replica of these Indices will generate returns equal to the return generated by this index. As the stocks are amongst the most liquid stocks in this Indices thus it will be very easy to liquidate positions at any point in time without losing much on the difference between the bid and ask price.

These indices have stocks representing various sectors. In the case of NIFTY 50, the financial sector has the highest weightage with 38% representation, followed by IT having 16.77% weightage.

You can also create your portfolio by selecting stocks from the list and assigning your chosen sectoral representation depending upon your assessment and risk appetite.

For example; if you feel that in the coming years, the performance of the Telecom sector is going to outshine other sectors then instead of 1.97% representation in NIFTY 50 you can create a portfolio with 4-5 % representation of the sector.

A portfolio can be created with a mix of Large Cap, Small Cap, Mid Cap stocks. In a falling market scenario, the small-cap & mid-cap stocks tend to fall more because of the inherent perceived risk in these stocks. Thus, only a very high-risk-oriented investor should create a portfolio having only small-cap stocks. Generally, the institutional investors with properly laid down portfolio management guidelines have a higher share of large-cap stocks in their portfolio for want of safety of the principal amount.

When the portfolio scheme looks for a higher return, the portfolio manager has to include Midcap & Small Cap stocks in the portfolio. Remember the higher the risk the higher is the probability of gain but at the same time the higher the risk the higher is the probability of losing all or a significant amount of principal in the downward market.

Similarly, we can create thematic/sectoral portfolios by using the stocks used to create thematic/sectoral indices. But the risk gets concentrated when you invest all or the majority portion of your money in a single theme or sector and if that sector faces some problem, then your portfolio will also reflect it by way of loss of capital/returns.

It is better to create a diversified portfolio containing stocks of companies from different sectors of the economy. Diversification helps in reducing risk. When the broader market falls, irrespective of sector majority of the stocks fall but it has been seen that diversification helps in reducing loss. Further Large Cap stocks with inherent value fall less in comparison to the mid-cap or small-cap stocks.

You can create different portfolios by using the above indices. For example, if you wish to confine yourself to the top best-performing stocks then you can choose the stocks chosen to create NIFTY Quality 30. Similarly, you can try with various parameters like stocks with higher dividend percentages, stocks with low volatility, stocks with high beta, etc.

Beta Stocks

Stocks that are highly volatile and have a high degree of responsiveness to all market fluctuations are called high beta stocks. High beta stocks increase or decrease in value much more in comparison to low beta stocks when the market moves.

Beta is the coefficient of variation of a stock demonstrating the rate at which the value of security changes in response to market movements.

Types of Beta Stocks

Beta >1

Stock with a beta value greater than 1 implies a high degree of responsiveness with the share market. Such stocks are expected to deliver substantial returns in a rising market. But at the same time, there is a risk of substantial loss in case of a falling market scenario.

These are generally small & mid-cap companies' stocks.

Beta=1

Stock with a beta value equal to one implies a nearly parallel impact on the share price in relation to the fluctuation in the benchmark market index. Generally, large-cap companies with sound financials have a beta value of 1.

Beta <1

In the case of stocks with a beta value less than 1, the stock does not fluctuate equally to the index or broader market thus providing stability. In the case of a falling market, such stock falls less, and also in the case of a rising market they do not rise quickly.

Beta is a crucial factor in creating a portfolio.

Trading Volumes

Knowing the trading volumes helps in differentiating liquid vs illiquid securities. There is no fun in investing in security that you cannot sell at the market price at the time you wish to. Thus, we need to keep ourselves away from illiquid securities. You can think of investing in illiquid securities, only when you are fundamentally convinced about the future potential of a company and are investing for a long period. Remember as a general principle you should avoid illiquid securities.

Volume measures the number of shares/derivatives contracts traded in the stock exchange. It is an indicator of market strength.

By tracking trading volume an investor can ascertain how much of a given stock has traded in a given period, this, in turn, will help him to take a calculated call on the movement of the stock.

If the share price is increasing with an increase in volumes, it will indicate that the traders are building positions on the buy-side and thus there are good chances that the stock will further go up.

Similarly, if the share price declines with the increase in the volume, then it indicates that short positions are getting built up in the stock. A short-term investor needs to remain on the side of the majority of the market participants to avoid losses.

Further, if the prices are peaking up, but volumes are decreasing then it can be an indicator for reversal of a trend. Above are general rules good for most of the time but not always.

By knowing about what other investors are trading, you can find out which stocks are going to move in a big way.

Analyzing volumes helps an investor in trend confirmation.

Trend Confirmation

If a market has to rise or fall it has to be accompanied by increasing volumes. A rising market will accompany rising volumes. Similarly, a falling market will also see rising volumes. In a rising market, the number of buyers will keep on increasing and the buyers' enthusiasm will result in increasing volumes on the buy-side which ultimately increases the share price.

In case of a stock fall with heavy volumes, it indicates that this is the time to recheck the fundamental position of the company. There should be a fundamental reason why all of sudden investors are moving away from the stock. Knowing the root cause of such a fall will help you to cut losses.

Bullish Momentum

If you witness an increase in volume on stock which was trading downward and now the stock price started moving higher. It might be followed by a downward move again but this time the downward move doesn't take the stock price below the previous low and the volumes on the downtrend also decrease then this move can be seen as a bullish sign and indicates that the stock prices are likely to move up.

Price Reversal

Increasing share price accompanied by decreasing volumes will indicate the market is losing strength and suggest a lack of interest in the stock and chances of reversal are increasing. Similarly, decreasing volumes in a falling market will indicate that the stock correction is about to complete and a reversal is nearby.

Volumes with Breakout

If a stock breakout from a technical range rises with the increase in volume, it indicates strength in the move but if the breakout is not supported by an increase in volumes or the volumes are falling then it indicates a false breakout, meaning the stock will retrieve back.

Any break of critical support or resistance level is not valid if the volumes are not increasing. Volume should move along with the trend.

Price	Volume	Interpretation
Rising	Increasing	Bullish
Falling	Increasing	Bearish
Rising	Decreasing	Bearish (trend reversal)
Falling	Decreasing	Bullish (trend reversal)

Volume preceded price

Generally, first, the volumes will increase before the prices start moving up or down. Thus, if an analyst tracks the volumes, then he will be able to anticipate the price movement. The spread between bid-ask will be narrower when volumes are higher because of an increase in liquidity.

These two indicators' prices and volumes need to be analysed together to get desired results.

Charles Dow, the founder of the Dow Jones, mentioned that volume confirms trends in price. He maintained that if a price was moving on low volume, then there could be many different reasons. But, when a price move was associated with high or rising volume, then he believed this as a valid move. If the price continued moving in one direction, and with associated supporting volume, then this was the signal of the start of a trend.

Value Investing

Value investing is an important investment strategy involving the selection of stock based on their intrinsic book value in comparison to the present market value. The chances of incurring loss are reduced to a greater extent when an investor chooses a stock with intrinsic value.

Many times, the market overreacts to good and bad news, resulting in significant movement in the stock price that does not correspond to the fundamental value of the company. During these overreaction times, investors get the opportunity to find stocks that are trading way below their intrinsic value and can invest in the stock after analyzing their fundamental position.

The market will never move continuously in one direction; it moves from extreme optimism to extreme pessimism. These are the times a value investor should watch out for. It is very important to buy the stock at a justified price because the higher the price you pay the lower will be the chance of you earning higher returns. The market runs on future expectations.

The concept of margin of safety introduced by Benjamin Graham in his book "The Intelligent Investor" is one of the core concepts of value investing. An investor should wait for the right opportunity and should never be in a hurry to buy stock. Sometimes a little rally in stock excites a trader and he jumps in to take part in the rally, this strategy is called riding the momentum but a value investor with mid- long-term focus should restrain and first analyse the true value of the stock and if he finds the present market value is near or lower than that then only, he should invest in such stocks.

The return on your investment is directly proportional to the efforts you have put in to understand the fundamentals of the stocks and find out the hidden value. The more time you devote towards increasing understanding and doing research, the more will be your returns. There can be some exceptions but in most of the situations, this rule will stand correct. The other aspect apart from the above is your behaviour which will come in between your capacity to generate returns and your actual returns. We will discuss the impact of behaviour on investing in detail in subsequent chapters.

The intrinsic value of Stock

It is very important to know what is the actual worth of a stock before investing in it. The current market price is a factor of market sentiments and thus might not reflect the true value of a stock. In a positive sentiment period, many investors will be chasing the stocks and thus the stock prices might be overvalued, and investing at this time might result in substantial loss.

Similarly in a pessimism sentiment period, the stocks might have corrected significantly as the stockholders are unwinding their position because of panic but the fundamentals of the company are far better than the prevailing market price and thus there are great chances of the stock bouncing back. This is the time to start investing in such fundamentally strong stock to gain from the subsequent bounce back.

An investor should use intrinsic value assessment to find out fundamentally strong stocks that are trading for less than their intrinsic value. In any business/trading the simple formula of earning money is to buy low and sell high. The intrinsic value calculation will assist you in determining whether you are actually buying the stock at a low price or not and also is there any growth potential.

The intrinsic value of a stock is its fair value. It can be calculated using the following methods

Discounted Cash Flow Method

Discounted cash flow analysis involves three steps.

- Estimate all of a company's future cash flows.

- Calculate the present value of each of these future cash flows.
- Sum up the present values to obtain the intrinsic value of the stock.

Estimating a company's future cash flow requires an understanding of the company's business model, its past financial performance, its competitors, the overall market scenario & the market scenario for the segment this company is representing. So, you can say it's assumptions with the use of common sense and fundamentals of the company.

To start with, first, have an understanding of the companies past few years' cash flows, it will give you a fair idea of the probable trends subject to the changes the company is proposing coupled with general growth prospects of the company in the coming years. The formula for calculating intrinsic value using discounted cash flow analysis is:

Intrinsic value = (CF1)/(1 + r)^1 + (CF2)/(1 + r)^2 + (CF3)/(1 + r)^3 + ... + (CFn)/(1 + r)^n

where:

- CF1 is cash flow in year 1, CF2 is cash flow in year 2, etc.
- r is the rate of return you could get by investing money elsewhere (you can take risk-free returns i.e., Government securities rate of return) or you can also use the cost of capital for discounting.

The detailed steps involved are

- Take the free cash flow of year one (you can also use the average of the last three years' cash flow) and multiply it with the expected growth rate.
- Project the cash flows for the next 10 years
- Discount all the next 10 years cash flows by choosing a

discount rate r
- Add up all the NPV of the free cash flows
- We are assuming that the 10th year company will liquidate as we cannot assume a company to be lasting forever. Further assuming cash flow beyond 10 years is going to be very difficult because of the uncertainties involved. We assume that the company will sell off its assets at the end of the tenth year at a sell-off valuation (residual value). For that purpose, we will use a multiplier of 12 for the tenth-year cash flow to simulate the value of these cash flows assuming the company would sell all its assets.
- Multiply the 10th year with 12
- Add up the values from steps 4, 5,6, and Cash & Cash Equivalents to arrive at the intrinsic value for the entire company.
- Now divide this value of discounted cash flow with the number of shares outstanding to arrive at the intrinsic value per share.

You can download intrinsic value calculators available on various internet websites for free and can use them to work out the intrinsic value using the DCF method.

Calculating Intrinsic value using EPS & P/E

Another easier method to calculate the intrinsic value of a stock is by using the P/E ratio

Intrinsic value = Earnings pcr share (EPS) x $(1+r)^n$ X P/E ratio

In the above formula

EPS= (net income-preferred dividend) / number of outstanding shares.

P/E Ratio: Current stock price / EPS

r= Expected earnings growth rate

n=Year for which you are working the intrinsic value.

As we are working out the future potential of the stock so we can use forward PE and forward EPS also instead of the last year's PE and EPS.

Let's calculate the Intrinsic value of Maruti Suzuki stock using the above formula as of 29th April 2021 as on date.

EPS=145

P/E Ratio=45.2

Rate of Growth =4.09%

n=1

Intrinsic value = Earnings per share (EPS) x (1+r) X P/E ratio

    = 145 X (1.0409) X 45.2

    = 6822

Book Value = 1738

Current Market Price = 6565

2. Calculate intrinsic value of Tata steel BSL

EPS =23

P/E Ratio=2.79

Rate of Growth=12%

n=1

Intrinsic value =Earnings per share (EPS) x (1+r) X P/E ratio

$$=23 \times (1.12) \times 2.79$$

$$=71.87$$

Book Value =192

Current Market Price = 69.85

Asset-based valuation

Another simple way of calculating the intrinsic value of a stock is by subtracting the company's liabilities from its assets

Intrinsic value = (Sum of company's assets) - (Sum of company's liabilities)

Here assets consist of both tangible and intangible assets. The value that arrived when divided by the number of shares outstanding will give the intrinsic value of the stock.

This method has its restrictions as growth prospects of the company are not taken into consideration while arriving at the asset or liability base and thus the intrinsic value arrived using this method will be on the lower side i.e., more conservative.

Benjamin Graham's intrinsic value formula

Benjamin Graham popularly known as the father of value investing has given the formula to find out the intrinsic value of a stock.

Intrinsic value = [EPS × (8.5 + 2g) × 4.4]/Y

In this formula

- EPS= Earnings per share of trailing twelve months is the average PE base for a no-growth company
- G is the reasonably expected growth rate in the next 7-10 years
- 4.4 is the average yield of AAA-rated corporate bonds in 1962 ((Graham did not specify the duration of the bonds, though it has been asserted that he used 20-year AAA bonds as his benchmark)- Source Wikipedia.
- Y is the current yield of AAA-rated corporate bonds.

Investors have the opportunity to invest the money in a relatively safer AAA-rated bond and thus the return on equity which is comparatively riskier should be calculated in relation to the risk-free (high degree of safety) rate of return. By dividing the current yield on AAA-rated corporate bonds the 4.4 percent bond rate is normalized to today's environment.

Tweaking the formula as per Indian markets

In the above formula instead of 4.4 percent, AAA-rated US-based corporate bond yield as the average yield we can use the average yield on 5 years fixed deposit in the Indian scenario. This can be taken as approx. 5%. Similarly, the average PE for no growth company can be different for Indian stocks but we will keep the same value here for our calculations.

You can work out the intrinsic value of any Indian stock and the relevant data i.e., EPS, the Growth rate can be obtained from the free website **www.screener.in**[1].

Let's calculate the intrinsic value of Maruti Suzuki as on 29th April
2021

EPS =145

Growth rate=4.09%

Yield on 10 years AAA rated Corporate Bond =6.053

Fixed deposit return for 5-year FD =5%

Intrinsic value = [EPS × (8.5 + 2g) × 4.4]/Y

= [145 x (8.5 +2x4.09) x 5] / 6.053

=1997

Book Value =1738

Present Market Value = 6573

It does not mean that you should wait till the stock price of Maruti cor-
rects itself to 1997 but if at any point of time you witness such price
during a correction then Maruti will be a very good value investing opportunity subject to other fundamentals remaining promising.

2. Calculate intrinsic value of Tata steel BSL

EPS =23

Rate of Growth=12%

Yield on 10 Years AAA rated Corporate Bond = 6.053

Fixed deposit return on 5-year FD =5%

---

1. http://www.screener.in

Intrinsic value= [EPS × (8.5 + 2g) × 5]/Y

= 23 x (8.5+2x12) x 5/6.053

=617

Book Value =192

Current Market Price = 69.85

With the above example, it is very clear that this formula cannot be used as a thumb rule as various other factors need to be considered while deciding to invest in a stock.

It can be seen that Benjamin Graham's formula is very conservative and there is a huge difference in intrinsic value in comparison to the intrinsic value arrived using the EPS & P/E formula.

Margin of safety

The difference between intrinsic value and the current market price of the stock is the margin of safety. The greater the margin of safety the safer will be the investment.

** Though the market participants use Benjamin Graham's formula to arrive at the intrinsic value of a stock but surprisingly, Benjamin Graham has never advocated using this formula as a thumb rule. He had suggested seventeen different rules in his book to identify stock for investing. Some of the key measures advised by him were

- Company with a diverse source of income.
- Adequate Size of company. Should not invest in too small a company.
- Strong financial conditions
- Earning Stability

- Dividend payment record
- Earnings growth
- Limiting your investment to stocks with a moderate P/E ratio
- Limiting your investment to stocks with a moderate price to book ratio

Going by the concept of margin for safety at present out of two stocks discussed above, Maruti Suzuki vs Tata Steel BSL, Tata Steel BSL seems to be more promising with higher intrinsic value.

The intrinsic value of options

Intrinsic value = (Stock price - Option Strike Price) X Number of options

Suppose you wish to trade on a stock of ABC corporate and wish to arrive at its options intrinsic value to take a call on whether the option is in the money or out of money. Let's assume the stock's present market value is $20 per share and you wish to buy five call options that entitle you to buy 100 shares of this stock @ $18. The intrinsic value of these options will be

($20-$18) x 500= $1000

But in this process the premium you have already paid needs to be subtracted to find the actual intrinsic value. We will discuss options trading in subsequent chapters.

Historical Trends

Historical trends are very important for an investor. There is a common saying "History repeats itself" and in the stock market, it is true most of the time. There are significant bull runs followed by financial crises resulting in significant crashes in the market. It has happened in the past and rests assured you will find such moments in the future also. A falling market represents panic in the public and after every panic selling, you will witness the wave of optimism revive and thus revive the upward trend again.

These moments of panic selling are an opportunity to collect quality stocks with high intrinsic value in comparison to prevailing market value. If you invest in such stocks after doing basic fundamental analysis, you are certainly going to make money in this market.

The market does not move in a single direction. It has its bull and bear market cycles. Each bull market is followed by a bear market. The trend could be short-term or long-term. By analyzing the historical trends an investor can anticipate future trends and can make investment decisions accordingly.

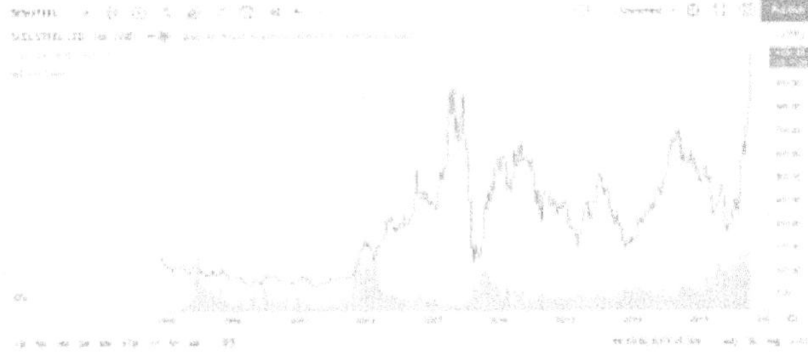

If you observe closely the above chart of TATA STEEL, you can make out that the stock has rallied significantly and a correction is due anytime. Thus, taking a long position at this point is very risky. A short-medium term investor until confident of the fundamental value in the stock at the present price should never enter at these levels.

Nobody knows in the present rally how far this stock will rise thus if as a tactical trader you wish to encash this opportunity, you can ride the momentum but with tight stop loss to avoid any significant loss.

Behavioural Aspects

Patience & discipline are two key behavioural aspects that determine a trader's/investors success in the stock market.

Assume we have taken a position in the stock market after convincing ourselves of the company's fundamentals, immediately after taking a position we get tempted to look at the screen more frequently with the hope of achieving a yearly target in intraday or maximum in 2-3 days. In this situation, if the stock falls a little bit, we get panic and in panic, we forget all the fundamental analysis done by us and cut our position. In most such cases once we cut our position the stock started rising and then we will not have the courage to enter the trade again.

The above scenario sounds foolish but it happens with most of us and the reason behind this is a lack of patience and discipline.

We know how the big banks or financial institutions maintain their position. They have strict policies in place and they act only when the stop loss or take profile targets are triggered. Further, they also have a detailed laid down mechanism of identifying the stocks and the risk mitigation. Their approach is a disciplined and policy-driven approach and the same can be replicated by retail investors also to make money out of this market.

Our behaviour determines our success in the stock market. There are plenty of stocks that either move up or go down daily, so it's not the stock or not our bad luck, it's our behaviour that determines the result.

It's a human habit to blame destiny or bad luck or others for all his failures but the root cause of most of the failures lies within us. I agree there will be a small percentage of cases where we can't do anything and its destiny that decides but I can assure you, those are very few incidences out of a total number of incidences in our life and in most of the cases we can control our destiny by realigning our behaviour (particularly in the stock market or financial planning).

Every failure is a building block of success in the future if we have failed today than it is because of our lack of discipline and if we continue to learn from our failure then success is not far away.

Another crucial aspect is learning. Keep learning different concepts of the stock market and with every learning, you will become wiser and wiser to take informed and calculated decisions. Learning from failure is good but it all depends upon how big the failure was. Sometimes stock market failure is too big to absorb and many investors never return to the market after one big failure. It's better to learn first than to learn by failures.

Enthusiasm is another behavioural aspect that is required for every success in the material world but in the stock, market enthusiasm can lead to disasters. The habit of being carried away can lead to big failures. Example: You have invested in a stock of a company after doing fundamental research, your investment decision has also turned right and the stock started rallying. You get carried away with such stock rise and did not book profit despite the stock surpassing your targeted price in hope of getting higher returns but then on one fine day when you get up from bed you got the news that a big financial crisis has gripped the entire world and the markets have opened with a huge gap. Your chosen share opened below your purchase price and straight away hit the lower band. This lack of discipline and over-enthusiasm has converted possible gain into a loss.

Similarly, many investors get carried away by the advice of other stock market gurus without doing their proper analysis. They invest huge amounts in the so-called stock market tips. This is a disaster in waiting for investors. Such decisions can wipe out your entire capital.

When the stock market is in a bull phase, you will find many stock market experts will emerge from the woods and start advising on stocks. Even many spam messages advising investing in particular sets of stock will also start filling your mobile's storage space. An investor needs to avoid getting carried away by this unwanted advice.

A prudent investor needs to learn that as the market rises the stock becomes riskier and riskier, thus investors need to book partial profit with every rise of the stock. Similarly, as the market falls the stocks become less risky and investors can start accumulating fundamentally strong stocks at every dip.

Our behaviour is something that stands in between our money-making from the market. Humans are a restless species and you also might have observed that it's very difficult even to sit silently in a room without doing anything.

This behaviour of humans is observed more commonly when you take a position in the stock market. After taking a position we become restless and start watching the screen more frequently resulting in panic selling even when the correction is only a normal movement or booking a very small profit when there is a potential for large gains. This is not investing, this is speculating.

To succeed in markets an investor needs to focus more on avoiding mistakes. $2/3^{rd}$ of your success depends upon avoiding mistakes and the remaining $1/3^{rd}$ on taking the right decisions. By avoiding mistakes an investor is improving his success rate and reducing chances of failures.

It sounds so easy, just to avoid mistakes and earn money but in reality, it's difficult to first understand if we are taking the wrong decision or not.

Its human behaviour to remain under the false impression that he is making the right decisions all the time and only when his decision goes wrong, does he realize that the decision was wrong. Still, at this moment, it's human nature to blame others, circumstances, etc for his failure, and accepting that his decision was wrong will come at last.

The easiest way to understand if your prospective investment decision is right or wrong is to ask questions to yourself. These questions can be on fundamental of the company you are identifying to invest in, market trend, present price vs expected price vs company valuations, etc. If you ask yourself, you will get clarity on taking such a decision.

Segregating stock market trading from emotions is a key to success. Trade without emotion and you will succeed whether as a speculator or investor. Emotional feelings, be it fear of losing, attachment with position, the false hope of recovery, etc, needs to be removed. Any trading decision should be detached from such emotions.

"All of the human unhappiness comes from one single thing: not knowing how to remain at rest in a room. - Blaise Pascal

Markets, Surprises & Insider Trading

———

Keeping lower expectations supports an investor in the right decision-making. Markets very rarely trade as per the expectation of an investor and always surprises them with wild moves. We have seen the coronavirus crisis in 2020. The world across the markets has fallen significantly and when everyone was afraid that it will fall further or it will take a long time to recover, the market surprised by registering a V-shaped recovery. In fact, in this recovery rally, the market has surpassed the previous peak.

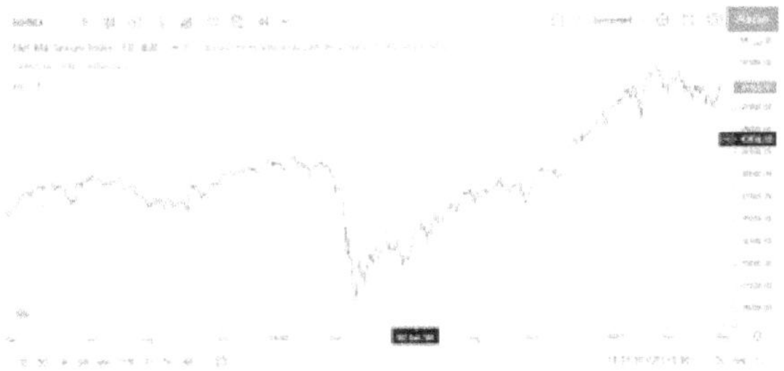

All this has happened without a significant change in fundamentals. The only change was the increase in positive expectations of the growth of the economy based on a lower previous year base.

It is very important to catch these moments to generate higher returns. When most of the public is negative on the markets, the markets were seen rising higher and when most of the public is positive on markets and expect it to go further higher, minor negative news leads the market to a significant fall.

There was a story of an industrialist selling unique goods in the market. His sales were not increasing even though his product was of use to the general public. He started thinking of ways to increase sales.

One day he got an idea to increase the sales and he started spreading rumours that his production is going to be slowed down and thus the product will be in short supply.

This sparked a demand for the product as everyone started expecting the prices of the product to go up and thus started accumulating more and more at lower prices.

The industrialist was very happy with the sales picking up, he gradually started increasing prices but the public, in general, started purchasing more as they were expecting prices to go up further.

After some time, the industrialist thought that the prices have increased substantially now let me buy back my product at a lower price, he spread another rumour in the market that there is another company coming in the market with a similar product.

The investors were now worried as the supply is going to surpass demand. They started dumping the products back to the industrialist or to anyone willing to buy at lower prices. The industrialist further kept on reducing the prices for this buyback and eventually repurchased a significant chunk at a much lower price than the price at which he has sold it.

This is insider trading.

A handful of people with knowledge of confidential but valuable information about the company plays with the market and makes money while the public, in general, becomes a victim of such incidences.

Indian markets are full of such insider trading examples. The penalty imposed by regulators is not adequate to stop this.

Inflation and the return

Inflation is the decline in purchasing power of a currency over time. Inflation results in the rise of the cost of goods and services thus the cost of living keeps on increasing making the returns received from the investment less worthy. The worth of Rs 100 today will not be the same 10 years in the future. With inflation, the worth of the money will reduce and you will not be able to buy the same amount of goods or services which you can buy today by paying the same price in the future.

A certain level of inflation is required in an economy to ensure that expenditure is promoted and hoarding of money is demotivated.

Particularly in the present market conditions (2020-21) when every major central bank is printing money or buying bonds of corporates/government to infuse liquidity into the system, it can be said with certainty that we are about to face a higher inflation period in the coming days. In such scenarios of excess liquidity more money is chasing the same good and thus the demand and supply equation is going to get impacted resulting in the price of goods and services increasing.

Assume you have invested in a certain asset category and are getting a yearly return of 6% but at the same time the prevailing inflation in your country is 5% then the actual return on your investment will be only 1% and not 6%. It's human nature that we feel getting a 6% return is good even when inflation is 5% and the actual return is only 1% against getting a return of 2% when inflation is 0%. This is termed by psychologists as a money illusion.

To overcome this crucial aspect impacting wealth creation an investor needs to find out avenues that can generate inflation-beating returns.

It becomes very important to invest in asset classes that can fetch inflation-beating returns if you wish to continue with your present standard of living in the future. Inflation is one of the key reasons, the equity market is a favourite investment avenue for most.

The share market has the potential to deliver inflation-beating returns. The other one could be inflation-linked bonds where the returns are linked with inflation rates. In countries like India, Real estate has proved itself to generate inflation-beating returns and that is the reason most Indians choose real estate for investment.

Further gold is also traditionally treated as a hedge against inflation.

Impact of Inflation on the Stock Markets

With the increase in prices of goods and services, the value of money decreases thus decreasing the purchasing power of investors. Inflation will leave less amount of investable money with the investor, resulting in investors shying away from the stock market triggering correction in the markets.

To tame inflation the central bank of the country will have to increase the interest rates on deposits and loans to suck excess liquidity from the system. This will encourage people to save more money with banks and curb excess liquidity.

Since loans also get costlier the purchasing power of investors on borrowed money reduces and the cost of capital for companies increases, thus companies prefer to defer the capital expansion plans, resulting in stagnation in growth which ultimately results in a correction in the market and lower equity valuations.

With the rising in inflation, the market will start expecting a drop in profitability of the companies due to higher borrowing costs both for goods and services as well as higher interest servicing costs on loans and advances. It triggers the selling in the share price leading to a market correction.

With a fall in profitability, the dividend income for investors also reduces thus triggering portfolio churning for the prudent investor. Value stocks are the least impacted ones in such scenarios as against the growth stocks.

Despite the above negatives, slight inflation is positive for an economy as prices rise at a normal rate encourages production and thus drives the economy. Further, a zero-price rise or negative price rise is known as deflation. Deflation is also negative for the economy as its currency will appreciate against the other countries' currency impacting its exports and discouraging manufacturing.

Thus, we must compare trends in inflation and compare it with past trends. If the rise in inflation is steady then it is good for the economy and stock market but if it is sudden then it is negative for both the economy and the stock market.

Real Estate Investment Trusts

A real estate investment trust commonly known as REIT is a company/trust that owns, operates, or finances income-generating real estate. It provides an easy way to invest in commercial real estate. Through REIT an investor can invest in income-generating real estate assets and can get benefited by

- Appreciation in the price of real estate assets.
- Earn a portion of rental income as a dividend.
- Diversification of portfolio.
- High liquidity despite investing in real estate assets.

- No need for investors to manage the real estate assets.
- Transparency as REIT is run by a Trust with disclosure requirements and regulated by a regulatory authority (In India, SEBI).
- Individuals can invest and acquire a portion of real estate assets with minimum contribution as against investing a large sum in acquiring physical real estate.

The investment in REITs is as simple as investing in any other share of a company. REITs also trade on the stock exchange and thus make it easier for investors to liquidate their position with ease.

REIT invests in a wide range of real estate properties including commercial offices, warehouses, hotels, malls, etc. They aim to generate rental income from the property along with price appreciation by leasing space and collecting rent on its real estate assets.

Before investing in a REIT an investor needs to be aware of the type of assets REIT has invested and the prospects of the rental income as well as price appreciation of the assets owned by the REIT. Generally, a REIT will invest in one single theme example: Commercial office space, etc. but they can choose to invest in a variety of real estate assets depending upon regulatory guidelines of the country as well as available mandates by the trust.

90% of the income generated by REIT has to be distributed to the shareholders.

The first REIT that came into existence in 1961 was American Realty Trust founded by Thomas J. Broyhill. It was established after the American government enacted legislation for REIT in 1960 through the Cigar Excise Tax Extension act to boost real estate development. Since then, many countries have adopted the concept of REIT and in India

REIT as an investment product has been introduced in 2007 & Embassy REIT is India's first publicly listed Real Estate Investment Trust.

In India at least 80% of the assets of REITs need to be completed and income-producing thus reducing the risk involved in underdeveloped property and the related cash flows.

REITs can be classified as Equity REITs & Mortgage REITs. Equity REITs hold properties such as commercial offices, hotels, shopping malls, etc, and generate most of their revenue from the rental income from these properties.

Mortgage REITs focus on financing properties and thus generating revenue from the interest earned on the investments made in mortgages or mortgage-backed securities. Mortgage REITs can finance both residential and commercial assets.

The percentage of an investor's investment in REIT depends upon individual risk appetite but it should be a part of the portfolio as it not only helps in diversification but also in generating stable dividend income with the opportunity for appreciation of capital.

Infrastructure Investment Trusts

Infrastructure investment trusts are introduced to promote the investment and development of the infrastructure sector. It pools money from several investors which in turn is used for investing in cash flow generating assets. Similar to REIT the cash flow generated is subsequently distributed to the investors as dividend income.

The basic difference between REIT and INvIT is the assets in which each one is mandated to invest. INvIT is mandated to invest in infrastructure assets like Roads, Bridges & other high-value infrastructural units as against REIT which invest in income-generating real estate assets such as commercial buildings, shopping malls, etc.

INvIT can raise funds both via public or private placement and in return, investors receive dividends and interests.

Generally, under construction assets are placed through private placement, and fully finished operational assets are placed through public offerings.

The sponsor company through INvIT deleverage itself by repaying its debt obligation as infrastructure projects take substantial time in generating adequate cash flows.

The benefits of investing in INvIT are

- Fixed income generation.
- Diversification of Portfolio.
- Liquidity despite investing in infrastructure projects.
- Professional management of diversified assets.
- Participation in high-value infrastructure projects with a minimum amount.

Inflation-indexed bonds/securities

The returns from any investment should be adequate to beat inflation. If inflation is higher in comparison to the returns generated then the returns in real terms will be negative as it is lower than the increase in the cost of living.

In India, RBI issued the past Inflation-indexed bonds but those were not very successful. Inflation-linked bonds were issued to provide security of capital and protection against inflation. The Government through RBI issues inflation-linked bonds from time to time and an investor can subscribe to those through open offers.

In general, investors should allocate at least 10% of their portfolio to long-term inflation-linked bonds/securities to safeguard the portfolio against rising inflation.

Exchange-Traded Funds

An Exchange-traded fund, ETF, is a marketable security that tracks an underlying asset. The underlying asset can be an index, a commodity, bonds, or even a basket of securities. Practically any asset class that has a published index and is liquid enough to be traded daily can be made into an ETF. The asset class can be Equity, Bonds, Real Estate, Commodities, Currencies, multi-asset funds, etc. In India NIFTY 50 ETF & Gold ETF are very popular investment tools.

ETF tracks the yield and return of the index or underlying to which it is mapped to. On buying a unit of an ETF, the investor is buying the portfolio to which the respective EFT is mapped. Example: If an investor wishes to have a return equivalent to NIFTY 50, he can simply buy an ETF that is tracking NIFTY 50 and the returns generated will be nearly similar to the return generated by NIFTY 50 over a given period.

To generate returns equivalent to NIFTY 50 index an investor instead of investing in all the portfolio stock which constitutes to form NIFTY 50 index and then tracking it regularly to implement and change in the percentage of weightage or constituent companies in NIFTY 50 for realigning its portfolio, it can simply subscribe to an ETF which in turn is investing in NIFTY 50 companies and is managed by professionals to generate similar returns.

ETFs are passively managed. The purpose of an ETF is to match the corresponding market index. The fund manager has to only do minor, periodic adjustments to realign the fund in line with changes in the corresponding index. The fund manager does not have the mandate to take investment decisions on his own, he has to simply replicate the corresponding index to generate similar returns.

Difference Between ETF & Mutual Fund

ETF trades like a common stock on a stock exchange and its price keeps on changing throughout the day just like any other stock. As against this Mutual fund trades on a NAV basis which is arrived daily after the closure of business. Thus, investment in an ETF is real-time as against in a Mutual fund it is delayed. The liquidity of the ETF is higher. For ETFs, investors need a Demat account but for a Mutual Fund, a folio needs to be created with the respective Mutual Fund.

Special Purpose Acquisition Company (SPAC)

A special purpose acquisition company is a shell company with no commercial operations. It is listed on a stock exchange to raise funds to acquire a private ltd company and thus making it public without going through the traditional route of IPO (initial public offering).

It is also known as a blank check company.

A SPAC is created specifically to raise funds to finance a merger or acquisition opportunity in a given period. SPAC will have a stipulated period (in US 2 Years) to complete the acquisition else they have to return the funds to investors.

SPAC is generally formed by investors having expertise in a particular sector and to push through the deals in their given sector. There is no need for the sponsor of a SPAC to declare their acquisition plans at the time of IPO. This saves sponsors from extensive disclosures required under the IPO process. The IPO investors will not have any idea of the company SPAC is targeting for acquisition and they have to trust the capabilities of the sponsors.

The funds raised by SPAC cannot be used for purposes other than acquisition or to return the money to the investor in case of liquidation of SPAC.

The record of SPAC as an investment tool is not encouraging and investors have generally lost heavily in high-value acquisition though sponsors have gained. The sponsors receive shares at a deep discount, so even when the price of the acquired company falls after the acquisition, the sponsors are still able to make decent profits.

Mutual Funds

A mutual fund is a trust that is entrusted with the responsibility to collect money from several investors with common investment objectives and invest the same in equities, bonds, money market instruments, etc and distribute the income generated from this collective investment proportionately amongst the investors after recovering applicable expenses & fees.

The money collected is managed professionally by a professional fund manager and is in line with the objectives of the scheme.

The investors' money is calculated based on "Net Asset Value" or NAV. NAV is the combined market value of the shares, bonds, and securities held by the fund on any particular day after adjusting for permitted expenses and charges. NAV per unit represents the market value of all the units in a mutual fund scheme after adjusting for expenses, liabilities, accrued income and is divided by the outstanding number of units in the scheme. Since the market value of securities changes every day, the NAV of the scheme also varies on a day-to-day basis.

Example of NAV: If the market value of securities of a mutual fund scheme is Rs500crore and the mutual fund has issued 10crore units of Rs 10 each to the investors, then the NAV per unit of the fund is Rs500cr/10cr=Rs50

Mutual funds are best for investors who

- Does not have expertise or willingness to trade in individual shares
- Lack large sums for investment

- Don't have inclination or time to research the market

Every mutual fund scheme is managed by a professional fund manager in line with the scheme's stated objective. The fund house charges a small fee for doing this service.

A passive investor has multiple product choices for investment across the different asset classes. Generally, investment in a mutual fund should be goal-oriented and thus the scheme should be chosen to align returns with your objective and time horizon.

Mutual funds are a great tool for diversification of your investment and thus reducing the concentration risk. But for meeting your objective the most important part is to select the right fund because the performance of active funds depends upon the fund manager's decisions.

Classification of Mutual Fund

Mutual funds can be broadly classified based on

- Organisation Structure- Open-ended, Close-ended, Interval
- Management of Portfolio- Active & Passive
- Investment Objective - Growth, Income & Liquidity
- Underlying- Equity, Debt, Hybrid, Money Market Instruments, Multi-Asset, Commodity
- Thematic / Solution-Oriented- Tax saving, Retirement benefit, Child welfare, Arbitrage
- Exchange Traded Funds
- Overseas Funds
- Fund of Funds

Organization Structure

Open-ended schemes

Open-ended schemes are perpetual and open for subscription and repurchase continuously on all business days at the prevailing NAV.

Close-ended schemes

Close-ended schemes have a fixed maturity date. The units are issued at the time of the initial offer and redeemed only on maturity. The units of close-ended schemes are listed on the stock exchange thus allowing investors to exit before maturity.

Interval schemes

Interval schemes allow purchase and redemption during specified transaction periods(intervals). The units of interval schemes are also listed on the stock exchanges.

Management of Portfolio

Active

In an Active fund, the fund manager is responsible to decide whether to buy, sell or hold the underlying securities. Investors expect active funds to generate higher returns in comparison to the passive fund. The performance of a fund depends upon the decisions taken by the fund manager.

Passive

Passive funds replicate an Index or benchmark like Index funds tracking the benchmark Index or Gold ETF tracing the movement in gold. The role of the fund manager in passive funds is limited and his decision of stock selection, buy, sell or hold is driven by the change in the benchmark Index. The objective of passive funds is to provide returns similar to the underlying benchmark with minimal tracking error.

Investment Objective

Growth

Growth funds are designed to provide capital appreciation. Primarily invested in equity. In the long-term equity as an asset class has traditionally outperformed most of the other investment classes. But in the short term, the portfolio returns can be volatile as equity is a volatile asset class. Investors should have a medium to the long-term horizon for investing in Growth funds.

Income

In the come fund aims to generate income at regular intervals. Thus, the investment will be in stocks that generate regular dividends, bonds, debentures, etc. Income funds mainly invest in fixed income securities.

Liquidity

The Liquid scheme aims to ensure the safety of funds with the return. It generally invests in short-term money market instruments like commercial papers, T-Bills, Government Securities, etc. These funds are ideal for investors who wish to park their surplus funds for a short period.

Underlying

Equity Fund

100% of the corpus in the Equity fund scheme will be invested in the stock market. Depending upon further classification, the investment can be into Blue Chip stocks, Mid Cap Stock, Large Cap Stock, Small Cap Stock, Thematic, etc. The risk will certainly be higher but at the same time, returns are also likely to be higher in comparison to other schemes over a period of time.

Debt

The investment in Debt mutual fund schemes will be into fixed income securities like Commercial Paper, Government Securities, Debentures, etc. The returns provided by these funds are relatively low in comparison to the Equity funds but at the same time risk will also be lower.

Hybrid

In Hybrid fund schemes, the corpus will be invested at a predetermined percentage in different asset categories. Mainly Equity & Debt. It provides the safety of debt funds along with higher returns of equity funds.

Money Market Instruments

The investment in this fund will be made into short-term money market instruments like Commercial Papers, T-Bill, Government Securities, etc.

Commodity

The corpus accumulated under this scheme is invested in underlying commodities like gold, oil, etc. The performance of the fund will be a replica of the performance of the underlying commodity except in cases where the fund is an active fund and the fund manager takes a call on the timings of entry and exit.

Overseas Funds

Overseas funds are those, which invest in equity, debt & equity-related instruments of companies listed outside India. Many of these funds are funds whose underlying funds invest in foreign markets. The corpus accumulated in this scheme is used to invest in ETFs based on the overseas equity market Index. It assists investors in greater diversification of portfolios and also to take advantage of the overseas stock market to generate higher returns. It also provides a hedge against domestic currency depreciation.

Fund of Funds

These funds do not directly invest in any stock or debt instrument but they invest in other mutual funds / ETFs to achieve diversification and return. The cost associated with these funds will be higher in comparison to other mutual funds.

Direct Plan Vs Regular Plan

In a direct plan of a mutual fund, investors invest directly without involving any distributor or agent. In a Regular plan, the investment is routed through a distributor or agent. The basic difference will be in the expense ratios and the availability of guidance.

The expense ratio will be lower in the direct plan in comparison to the regular plan as there is no distributor or agent involved.

Though both can have the same portfolio and fund manager but will have slightly different NAV.

Direct plans are for those categories of investors who have knowledge of mutual funds and are capable enough to choose a mutual fund scheme that can match their risk profile as well as meet their returns expectations. While in a regular plan a certified financial service provider will guide the investor about schemes that match the investor's criteria for investment and will assist the investor in investing.

In mutual fund investment, an investor can start with investment in Index funds. This will be a passive investment and returns will be in line with the performance of the Index. NIFTY Next 50 or NIFTY 50 can be a good option. Another relatively safer way to start mutual fund investment is to opt for Large Cap funds. The corpus will be invested in promising large-cap companies thus providing relative safety with the return.

Tactical Investing

Tactical investing is a short-term investment to gain from the short-term investing opportunity. Tactical investors identify a trend early and take a position to gain an advantage of the trend. It requires active participation by the investor to look for opportunities. Usually, technical analysis is used to find out entry and exit opportunities.

Along with the long-term investment, portfolio managers use tactical investing for a small portion of the portfolio to generate higher returns. The risk in tactical investing by using short-term technical indicators will be higher in comparison to long-term investment done after fundamental analysis.

Tactical trading can be done based on the short-term fundamentals of the company. For this, the investor needs to devote time to identify the opportunities.

Some of the common indicators for tactical investing is

1. Inflation data
2. Interest rate change
3. GDP, IIP, fiscal deficit, and other important economic growth data
4. Interest arbitrage
5. Movement of money from developed economies to emerging markets and vice versa.

Many investors who have time adopt a combination of long-term goal-based investing and tactical investing.

Momentum Buying

The momentum investing strategy is based on the perception that the market will continue to trend in the same direction till any significant fundamental change takes place to alter the trend. During this period the support and resistance will be driven by technical indicators and using these technical indicators a tactical investor can take a position with anticipation that the trend can persist for some time and investors can take benefit of it.

Under momentum investing an investor takes position in the same direction in which the market /stock is heading and rides the wave. This strategy requires strict adherence to the technical indicators that provide entry and exit points.

The credit for momentum investing goes to fund manager and businessman Richard Driehaus.

In the above chart of ITC, when the 50-day moving average crosses 200 days moving average from the top the downward trend is set. Similarly, when the 50-day moving average crosses the 200-day moving average from the bottom, an upward trend has started. Using these early indicators, an investor can take a short-term position and ride on the momentum wave.

The above is only an example of technical indicators, you can work out many more indicators. Some of which we will discuss in due course.

Risk in equities

Risk of losing capital

Equity is subject to a high degree of risk and investors should not invest in the equity unless they are prepared to take the risk of possible loss of capital. This risk can be reduced but cannot be fully eliminated. The risk mitigation will involve concepts like value investing, stop loss, diversification, etc.

Liquidity Risk

Liquidity in equity investment depends upon the trading volumes and settlement periods. Liquidity is important as it determines the chances of the investor getting the market rate while unwinding the transaction. The difference between the bid-ask rate should be minimum.

Trading volumes are generally high enough in large-cap securities but the situation can change all of a sudden with one big negative or positive news. With big negative news, stock can start hitting lower bands and thus holders of the equity share will not get a chance to liquidate their position. Similarly, small-cap and many mid-cap stocks lack liquidity even without any big news is a concern.

As a thumb rule, an investor should avoid dealing in illiquid stocks until and unless it has very high potential and the investor is willing to keep invested for a long-term horizon.

Event Risk

The change in the price of equity shares due to certain company or sector-specific events. For example; news of a big company's auditors suddenly resigning stating issues related to corporate governance can take the stock price of this company & in turn the investor's investment into deep trouble.

Risk in debt securities

Are bonds safe?

This is the question that comes to investors' minds when they have to take a call. Bonds were traditionally considered safer than equities but is it always true?

The safety of your investment lies in the nature of the bonds and the company/corporation floating the bonds.

Bonds are instruments issued by companies to raise funds from the markets and thus it is a debt. This debt has to be repaid by the company along with interest. This will be possible only when the company will continue to do good in the future and generate enough revenue to meet this repayment obligation.

This revenue-generating capability depends upon various factors impacting the business, it can be the general economic scenario, the product obsolescence, the pricing, the competition, the demand and supply matrix, change in regulations, etc.

If repayment of debt is easy then no bank would have failed but we can see, history is full of bank failures.

There is one exception and that is bonds issued by sovereign governments to raise funds from the market. Government bonds are treated by the market as the least risky because they are backed by government undertaking to pay on maturity and the government has the power to print money.

In this case, also, we have examples of countries where the currency devaluation/inflation is such that the bonds have no value when they were due for maturity. What will an investor do if a bond worth $1000 on maturity is fetching $1500 but the currency exchange rate or inflation in that economy has worsened beyond that?

History is full of incidences when the sovereign governments have been crippled in meeting their debt obligation.

In the 1960s & 70 Latin American countries, Mexico borrowed a significant sum of money from international creditors / US Banks for the development of infrastructure in their countries. As the economies of Latin American countries were doing good and at the same time the interest rates in developed economies were very low, to gain better returns, investors/banks poured in money by subscribing to debt instruments issued by these sovereign governments.

Mexico borrowed against future oil revenues. All these debts were borrowed in US $ and when the interest rates in the US started increasing to check the domestic inflation, the world entered into recession hitting oil market collapse, this eventually resulted in the collapse of the economy of Mexico & other Latin American countries.

A similar situation is going on now also (2020-22), after subprime crises of 2007-8, the US & other developed economy have kept their interest rates way too low, this has fuelled the movement of cheap money from developed economies to underdeveloped or developing economies for want of higher returns, resulting in a jump in stock markets in developing economies and ballooning of debt markets in these economies. Now with the slightest indication of an increase in interest rates in the developed economy the markets in developing economies are getting spooked.

Thus, it can be said that bond is also risky but are traditionally seen as less risker than equities. In this chapter we will discuss some of the key risks a debt instrument has;

Interest rate risk

In a rising interest rate scenario, the price of fixed income securities falls, and in a falling interest rate scenario the price of fixed income securities increases. This is because of the movement of investment from low-interest-paying bonds to other avenues for generating higher returns in case of rising interest rate scenario and movement of investment from other avenues to fixed income securities in a falling interest rate scenario.

Inflation and the accompanying central bank's action on the interest rate to control inflation are key events to watch if you have an investment in fixed income securities i.e., bonds, debentures, government securities, money market instruments, etc.

Credit Risk

The risk that is associated with default by the issuer in payment of interest or principal on the bonds/debentures is termed as credit risk.

Government bonds are the safest bonds as they are backed by a sovereign guarantee and thus have the lowest credit risk. In comparison to Government all the other bond/debenture issuers i.e., corporates are having a risk higher than the Government bonds and thus will be sold at a higher yield. Because of this higher risk, the spread on corporate bonds will certainly be higher than the government bonds and in a stressed scenario the spread on corporate bonds keeps on increasing. This increase in the spread can be termed as spread risk.

Liquidity Risk

L iquidity risk refers to the ease with which securities can be sold at their true value. Liquidity conditions keep on changing for bonds depending on the market conditions. In case a credit risk crystallizes the liquidity risk also increases for that particular instrument. In India, the 10-year G-Sec is the most liquid fixed-income security. But other government bonds are not so liquid and the trading volumes in other benchmarks are much lower in comparison to 10-year G-Sec.

Counterparty Risk

C ounterparty risk arises when one of the parties in the transaction fails to deliver security/consideration.

Prepayment Risk

I n case a corporate chooses to liquidate its obligation towards bonds before maturity then the bondholder will have a risk as he will have to again realign his portfolio to match the desired return. Generally, in a falling interest rate scenario, the bond issuer will like to prepay the existing bonds so as to float fresh bonds at lower yields.

Reinvestment Risk

T he coupon earned on fixed income securities may or may not be reinvested at the same interest rate and thus give rise to reinvestment risk. Similarly, if a bond matures the fund manager has to invest the bond proceeds in some other fixed-income instrument that may or may not deliver a similar return. Thus, investment is subject to reinvestment risk.

How to invest?

Lump-Sum

Lump-Sum investment is investing a big amount as and when the investor is having a surplus. In the case of Lumpsum investment timing and proper analysis of the stock is very important, else there is a high chance that the lumpsum investment will result in loss.

For example, an investor has invested a sizable amount when the market has already rallied then there is a significant risk that the market will witness correction and thus erosion in value for the investor.

Making money in the market is not easy and it requires discipline and patience. It has been seen many times that once an investor has invested his money the market either falls or continues to trade in a narrow band for quite a long time and when the investor cuts his position either in loss or with a small gain, the market again bounces back.

Did the market wait for investors to cut his position?

No, it's a lack of patience and a disciplined approach in investing that results in this actual or opportunity loss.

Systematic Investment Plan

The best way to invest in the equity market is through a systematic investment plan. In this process, investors invest an equal amount of money at regular intervals (monthly, weekly, etc) irrespective of where the underlying share price is trading. When the share price is high, he receives a smaller number of shares but when the share price falls, he receives a higher number of shares for the same amount. Due to this process, the average cost of borrowing or portfolio cost remains under control.

SIP enables investors to lower the average cost of investment and reduce the risk of investing at the wrong time.

SIP enables an investor to regularly increase his investment amount by a fixed amount and get the benefit of compounding as the investor earns returns on the returns generated by his investment.

Example: Dividend income generated by equity will be automatically reinvested in the mutual fund thus giving the benefit of the power of compounding.

SIP can be less stressful in comparison to the lump sum investment in a volatile market.

Impact Cost

Impact cost is the cost of executing a trade in a stock for a given order size at any given point in time. It is a measure of market liquidity. It is the percentage mark-up paid while buying/selling the desired quantity of stock with reference to its ideal price i.e. (best buy + best sell) / 2

Let's work out the impact cost for a stock

You want to buy 1000 shares of XYZ company. The market order book of the share is

Buy Quantity	Buy Price	Sell Quantity	Sell Price
1000	152	700	153
500	151	1000	154

The ideal price for your trade to buy 1000 shares should be $(152+153)/2 = 152.50$

But as the sell quantity order is not adequate the actual trade will take place as

$(700 \times 153 + 300 \times 154)/ 1000 = 153.30$

Thus, impact cost for purchase of 1000 shares will be $(153.30-152.50) \times 100 / 152.50 = 0.52\%$

Technical Indicator

It is very difficult to predict stock market movement with accuracy as many times markets move irrationally.

In March 2020, when coronavirus hit the world, the financial markets across the globe crashed. On 10th Feb 2020, the NIFTY 50 was near an all-time high with a level of 12159 but within a month it has corrected by 4600 points and touched a low of 7511 on 23rd March 2020. Again, when the whole world was fighting with coronavirus and resultant lock-downs the stock market started rising silently and touched a peak of 15431 on 15th Feb 2021 i.e., within a year. This high was approx. 3000 points higher than the previous high.

How can you explain this?

Markets have rallied on the hope of vaccination, the huge liquidity infused by central banks across the world which finds its way to stock markets for want of higher returns and a strong rebound in the economy but many of us were not able to catch it.

For an investor, it is important to understand when the markets are overreacting and should take benefit of over pessimism or over-optimism.

Connecting every dot is important to ascertain the future trend of the market. That is the reason I have discussed the bond market at the beginning of the book. You need to have an eye on world financial happenings, political & strategic developments, commodity markets, foreign exchange markets, bullion, bond & debenture markets, money market, central bank actions to enable you to take calculated calls on the market direction. In today's interconnected world, an event in one part of the world can shake the stock market/bond market in the other part of the world.

But as an investor, you need to learn to take benefit of such opportunities rather than getting afraid of such events. Apart from fundamental news impacting price moments, some technical indicators are used worldwide to ascertain trends.

Support & Resistance

You might have heard of support and resistance in equity trading. Support and resistance are nothing but the price at which a high number of traders are willing to take a bet in anticipation that the equity share price will not breach these levels. The reason for this belief could be any technical point i.e., it could be Fibonacci retracement level, it could be support line or resistance line, it could be double top or double bottom, etc.

Support represents the low level a share price reaches over time and bounces back from these levels. At this level, traders are willing to buy as they think that stock will not go below these levels. This collective buying by several traders results in stock prices stop dropping further and start rising. When the number of sell orders is higher in comparison to buy orders, the support level breaches indicate that the collective market opinion is negative on the stock and the stock is likely to drop further, generally, the breach of support is accompanied by negative news on the underlying stock or broader market/sector.

Resistance level represents the high level a share price reaches overtime but could not sustain above these levels and fall below the resistance level. Resistance level indicates that a large number of traders are of the view that stock is overvalued at these levels and is unlikely to sustain at these levels or rise above these levels. Thus, a lot of sell orders will be placed at resistance levels. A significant breach of resistance level indicates a change in market opinion on the stock and now the majority of the traders are bullish on the stock.

Trend Line

One way you can find support and resistance levels is by drawing imaginary lines on a chart that connect the lows and highs of a stock price. These lines can be drawn horizontally or diagonally. It can be seen from the below chart of NIFTY 50 that the stock reacts to the support line and whenever it reaches the support line the stock price bounces back, similarly whenever the stock price touches the upper band i.e., resistance line the stock price is corrected.

This support and resistance are nothing but the cumulative opinion of the majority of the market participants that stock will react at these levels. With this anticipation, the market participants built their position and the stock reacted accordingly. Generally stock respects these levels but when accompanied by big fundamental news it breaks these levels and forms a new trend line with new support and resistance levels.

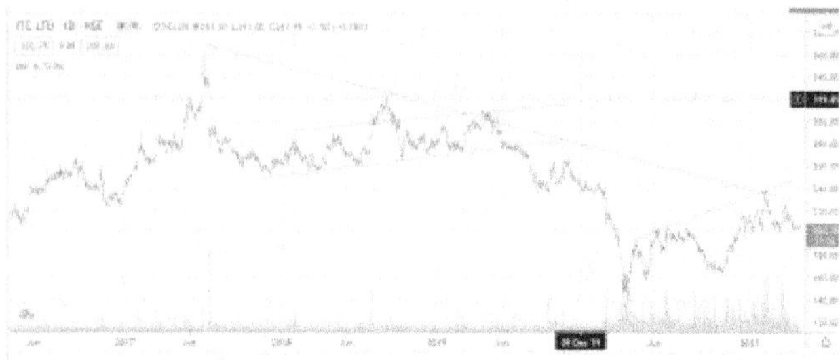

There can be several small trends within a large trend.

Fibonacci Numbers

The credit for the discovery of Fibonacci numbers goes to Leonardo Pisano Bogollo, an Italian mathematician from Pisa. He has illustrated this concept in the 12th century.

The Fibonacci number series is a sequence of numbers in a series such that the value of any number in the series is the sum of the previous two numbers.

0, 1, 1, 2, 3, 5, 8, 13, 21, 34, 55, 89, 144, 233, 377, 610, 987, 1597,

It can be seen from the above series that every number is a summation of the previous two numbers

5=3+2

21=13+8

377=144+233

Another interesting property of the Fibonacci series is if you divide any number of the Fibonacci series by its previous number the ratio will be approximately 1.618

For example:

21/13=1.6154

34/21=1.619

144/89=1.618

377/233=1.618

610/377=1.618

The ratio of 1.618 has its connection to nature, it can be found in flower petals, human faces, etc. You can get more information on the same in Wikipedia. Further, if we divide a number in the series by its immediately succeeding number the ratio will be 0.618

377/610=0.618

233/377=0.618

89/144=0.618

This 61.8% is a very important level in Fibonacci analysis.

If we divide any number in the Fibonacci series by a number two place higher than we get

For example:

55/144=0.382

89/233=0.382

233/610=0.382

38.2% is another crucial level in Fibonacci analysis

Another consistency can be found when a number in the Fibonacci series is divided by a number three places higher.

For Example

55/233=0.236

89/377=0.236

233/987=0.236

This 23.6% is the third important ratio in Fibonacci analysis.

Fibonacci Retracement gives an idea of where the stock will find support and resistance and can be used for tactical investment. As world across market participants are watching these levels and building positions, thus these levels play a crucial role in support and resistance.

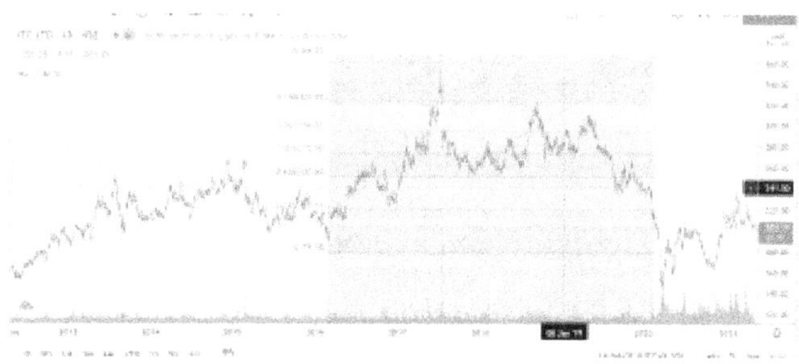

When we draw Fibonacci retracement from the low to high level or high to a low level, it will give the support/resistance levels for the subsequent movement of the stock. From the above chart of ITC, it can be seen that the stock reacts to the crucial Fibonacci retracement levels of 61.8%, 38.2% & 23.6%.

Knowing the Fibonacci level can help tactical investors in timing the entry and exit

Moving Average

Moving average is used to find the trend and to determine the support and resistance level of stock. It shows the average value of a stock price over a given period. The period can be 10 days, 20 days, 50 days, 200 days, etc. It is usually plotted along with the closing price.

Moving average indicator negates the short-term fluctuations thus enabling the user to identify the underlying trend. The most commonly used moving averages are;

Simple Moving Average & Exponential Moving Average

The security price is compared with the moving average price to understand the opportunities for trading. A rising moving average shows the prices are generally increasing, while a falling moving average indicates prices are falling.

When the security price rises above its long-term moving average it indicates a buy signal & when the security price drops below the long-term moving average it's a sell signal.

Another strategy adopted is to compare the short-term and long-term moving average, when the short-term moving average crosses above the longer-term moving average, it indicates a buy signal and when the short-term moving average crosses below the longer-term moving average it indicates a sell signal.

It is a lagging indicator as it gives signals based on past data. It should be used along with other fundamental and technical indicators to confirm the trend.

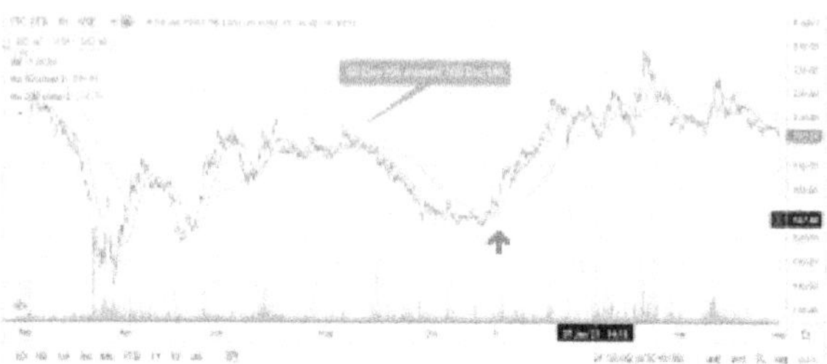

The simple moving average is calculated by adding the closing price of stocks for the given number of days and dividing it by the number of days.

Stochastic Oscillator

A stochastic oscillator is used to identify overbought and oversold signals. The stochastic oscillator moves in a range i.e., 0-100. Above 80 is considered as an overbought range and below 20 is considered as an oversold range.

A stock can continue to be overbought or oversold for a very long period thus this indicator can only give signals but to confirm the possibility of reversal, investors need to use it along with fundamental analysis & other technical indicators like moving average or Fibonacci retracement, etc.

The stochastic oscillator consists of two lines, one reflecting the actual value of the oscillator for each session and the other reflecting its three-day simple moving average. The intersection of these two lines is an indicator signal of a reversal. The divergence between stochastic oscillator and security price is also an indicator of reversal in process. During a bearish trend, if the stock is trading lower lows but the oscillator is indicating higher lows, it might be an indicator that sellers are exhausted and a reversal in trend is building up. The standard period used in a stochastic oscillator is 14 days.

The reading of the oscillator is worked out by calculating the high and low during these 14 days and then using the formula

(Current close price - 14-day low price) / (14-day high price - 14-day low price) *100

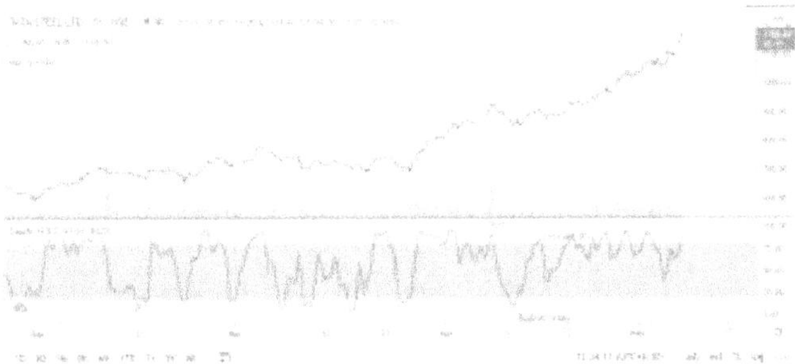

MACD

Moving Average Convergence Divergence indicator is an oscillator used to determine trends. It shows the relationship between two moving average indicators. The two lines in the oscillator cross each other giving a trading signal. MACD can be calculated by subtracting the value of a 26 day and 12-day exponential moving average. The shorter period exponential moving average constantly converges towards and diverges away from the longer EMA. This causes MACD to oscillate around zero level.

When MaCD crosses above zero it is considered as a bullish signal, while the crossing below zero is treated as bearish. Further, a turn-up of MACD from below zero level is considered as bullish and a turn-down from above zero is considered as bearish. When the shorter-term moving average crosses, the longer-term moving average from below it is treated as a bullish signal and when the shorter-term moving average crosses the longer-term moving average from above it is treated as a bearish signal.

Bollinger Bands

Three lines compose Bollinger Bands: A simple moving average (middle band) and an upper and lower band. The upper and lower bands are typically 2 standard deviations +/- from a 20-day simple moving average but can be modified.

It is believed by traders that the closer the price move to the lower band, the security is oversold and the closer the price move to the upper band, the security is overbought.

A period of low volatility is followed by a period of high volatility. So, if the width of the band is shrinking then it can be assumed that soon the volatility will increase resulting in the band expanding and prices shooting up or down.

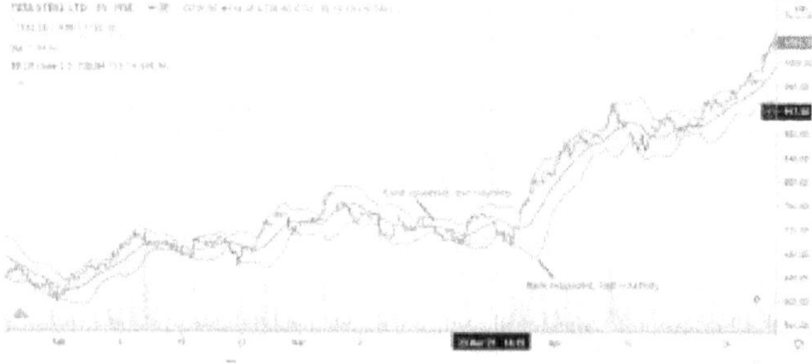

Relative Strength Index (RSI)

The relative strength index (RSI) is a popular momentum oscillator that goes between 0-100. The RSI provides technical traders with signals about bullish and bearish price momentum. An asset is usually considered overbought when the RSI is above 70% and oversold when it is below 30%.

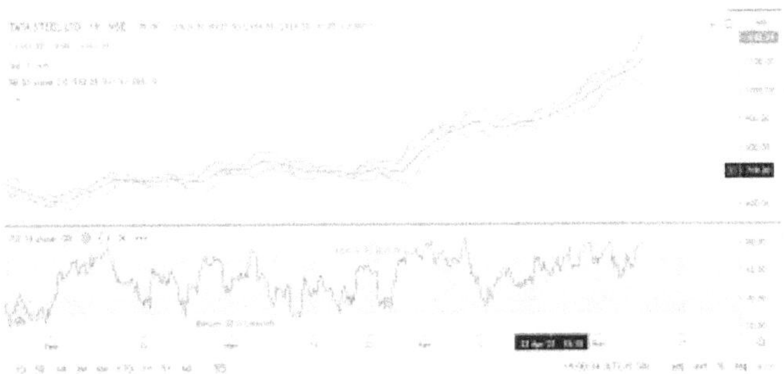

Corporate Action

Dividend

The dividend is the distribution of net income, after taxes, distributed to the shareholders. The company is under no obligation to declare and distribute dividends but as a matter of good corporate governance practice, most of the blue-chip companies distribute dividends from their annual profits. Companies can choose not to pay dividends and use the profit generated for future capital expansion.

The dividend is an additional income in the hands of investors and thus apart from the price appreciation of the stock, shareholders get benefit by receiving the dividend.

On the day dividend is to be distributed, most of the time the company stock reacts accordingly and adjusts its price in line with the dividend distributed. Example: If a share of face value 10 is trading at Rs 250 and a dividend of Rs 10 per share is announced, then generally the stock will open with a gap down to Rs240 on the date of dividend distribution. But exceptions are always there and it depends upon the strength of the company and market perception about the growth momentum of the company.

Stock Split

A company splits its stock so that a greater number of instruments can trade in the market. Example: A company's stock having a face value of Rs 10 is trading at Rs250. Now if the company splits the stock into a 1:2 ratio then for every one share, the holder will get one more share and the face value of the share will reduce from Rs10 to Rs5 per share.

Impact on the market value of the share will be visible on the day of split and the market price will open with a gap down to Rs125 as the stock is split into two. Though as an investor it will not impact you as your holding will get an increase from 1 share to 2 shares with a face value of Rs5 each and a market value of Rs125 each.

As prudent investors, we need to be careful on the stock split announcements, sometimes the stock behaves wildly on the day of the split and it gives a good opportunity to increase holdings or take fresh positions depending on the fundamental strength of the company.

Bonus

Bonus share does not reduce the face value of the share as these are additional shares allotted by the company to the existing shareholder. The market value of the share gets adjusted on the day the share trades ex-bonus.

Bonus share is a reward by the company to the shareholders. These are issued out of the reserves of the company and are free to the shareholders. These are allotted in fixed ratio ex: 2:1 means for every two shares the shareholder will receive one more share etc.

Let's try to understand it by an example of a 2:1 bonus

Pre-Bonus			Ex-Bonus		
Holding	Market price	Total Value of Investment	Holding	Market price	The total value of an investment
100	250	25000	150	166.67	25000

Bonus shares increase the liquidity position of shares and encourage retail participation as the share price has reduced enabling small investors to invest in these shares.

Right Issue

The right issue is a way to raise fresh capital but without going public. In this case, the company approaches its existing shareholders to raise fresh capital.

The right issue is subscribed by the existing shareholder in the proportion of their existing shareholdings. Example

1:5 right issue means for every 5 shares owned by a shareholder; he will be eligible to subscribe for an additional 1 share.

Now to make the offer attractive, the company generally issues new shares at a price lower than the prevailing market price.

The right issue can make sense as the new share is available at discount and can be offloaded immediately in the market. But again, an intelligent investor needs to understand the financial position and prospects of the company to take a calculated risk.

Buyback

A company buys back its share to consolidate its position. When a company has enough liquidity, it can choose to buy back the shares from the market. The company can choose to do so too;

consolidate the shareholdings from a wider base to selected few indicating confidence of promoters in the company's growth prospects.

Sometimes promoters offer buyback to avoid the company slipping away to a hostile takeover.

Another reason could be to support the share price and check the fall in the share price. It is a way promoter shows confidence in the company and expects the market to take a positive note of it and stop selling its shares at discount.

Buyback is generally treated as positive for share price because buyback is generally announced at a price higher than the prevailing market price or at market price and thus there is a scope for the market price of the share to go up.

Derivatives

A derivative is a financial instrument whose value is derived from the value of one or more underlying. These underlying can be stock, bonds, currency, commodities, etc.

The most commonly traded derivatives are

1. Forwards
2. Futures
3. Options
4. Swaps

Out of these Futures and Options are traded on stock exchanges.

Forward

A forward contract is a customized contract between two parties to settle a transaction at a pre-agreed rate on a given date in the future. Forwards is a right as well as obligation to undertake the transaction on the due date at the pre-agreed price.

Let's, understand forward by an example;

XYZ has entered a forward contract with you on 15th November 2021 to buy 100 shares of Amazon at a rate of \$3700 per share on 30th of November 2021.

On 30th November 2021, the scenario could be

Party	No of Shares	Market Price	Agreement Price	P&L
Buyer (XYZ)	100(B)	3600	3700	Loss of $100 per share
Seller (You)	100(S)	3600	3700	Profit of $100 per share

So irrespective of the market movement of the underlying between the contract start date and contract expiry date both XYZ and you are bound to settle the transaction @ $3700/Share on the due date.

The above transaction is an opportunity loss for XYZ as he could have bought @ $3600 per share if he has not entered into the agreement.

But if the share price of Amazon on 30th November 2021 could be above $3700 then XYZ would have the right to buy from you # $3700 per share and earn profit from the deal.

Forwards are the most common form of derivative used to hedge foreign exchange conversion risk and it is an over-the-counter product.

The main features of forward contracts are

- They are bilateral contracts and hence exposed to counter-party risk.
- Each contract is custom designed, and hence is unique in terms of contract size, expiration date, and asset type and quality.
- The contract price is generally not available in the public domain.
- The contract has to be settled by delivery of the asset on the expiration date or it can also be net settled.

In case a party wishes to reverse the contract, it has to compulsorily go to the same counterparty, which being in a monopoly situation can command the price it wants.

Futures

Futures are a standardized form of forward contract which is traded on an exchange. It is bought and sold on the exchange for a future delivery date at an agreed price. To make forwards traded on exchanges, the contract price and expiry dates are standardized. Thus, futures are traded in a multiple of the given lot size.

Exchange act as a centralized counterparty to both buyer and seller for future contracts and thus reduces the counterparty risk faced by forwards which is an OTC contract. Further, the liquidity position of the future contract will be very high in comparison to forwards, resulting in a very low spread between the bid and ask price.

Bid price is the rate at which the market is willing to buy a security/stock.

Ask price is the rate at which the market is willing to sell a security/price.

The difference between the bid and ask is termed as spread. For an illiquid stock, the spread will be high in comparison to liquid stock where the spread will be very low.

A higher spread makes it difficult for traders to offload their position at good market prices.

Stock futures is a highly leveraged position. It allows market players to trade on a particular security/stock/ commodity by investing only a small portion of the amount involved.

This high leverage results in a high gain or high loss depending upon the direction the stock is moving.

An investor needs to be very careful while dealing in futures as a little negative movement of underlying can result in very high losses.

The investor has to keep margin with stock exchanges through a stockbroker to take and keep their position in the future. The margin required to take the position is termed as Initial Margin.

Example: You wish to buy 100 shares of ABC Pvt Ltd which is trading at Rs100per share

The lot size of this script is 100 shares. Thus, the total position you are going to take by purchasing or selling one lot of ABC Pvt Ltd is

100 *100= 10,000/-

Let's assume the stockbroker/exchange charges an Initial margin of 10%, then you have to keep 10% of 10000 i.e., Rs100 with your stock broker for purchasing or selling one lot of futures of ABC Pvt Ltd.

Futures needs a daily mark to market settlement and thus, apart from the initial margin, the position holder has to make good for the MTM losses on daily basis.

Example: You have bought 100 shares of ABC Pvt ltd which is presently trading at Rs100 i.e., one lot by paying an initial margin of Rs1000 (10% of total value). Now the share price of ABC Pvt ltd has cracked down to Rs90/Share.

At the end of the day, your net position will be as under

Bought one lot of 100 shares @Rs100/- each=RS100x100=10,000/-

Present Market value =Rs100x90=9,000/- (as the share price has cracked down to Rs 90 from earlier Rs 100).

In this case, the initial margin alone will not be adequate as the broker will be at risk if the share continues to fall further. Thus, the stockbrokers will take an additional margin to cover such adverse movement in share price. This subsequent margin will be equal to the difference between your purchase price and the present market price and it is termed as Mark to Market Margin.

In this case, MTM will be Rs 1000/-

The basic terminology associated with future contracts is as under

Long Position: Number of unsettled purchase contracts held by the buyer.

Short Position: Number of unsettled sell contracts held by the seller.

Open Position: Unsettled long and short positions are termed open positions. Example

You have bought 3 future contracts of ABC Pvt ltd & sold 2 future contracts of XYZ ltd. In such a scenario your open position is 3 long on ABC & 2 short on XYZ.

Trade Volume: Total number of transactions traded in a given time frame. In the share market, it refers to the number of shares exchanged hands in a given period.

Open Interest: Open interest is the total number of outstanding derivative contracts that are not yet settled. A high open position in a bullish market indicates further momentum on the upside. Similarly, a high open position in a bearish market will indicate further fall on the downside.

Cost of carrying: Assume you have bought 100 shares of ABC Pvt. ltd for Rs 100 per share. Thus, you have invested a total amount of Rs 10,000/-

Assume you have taken a loan @ 6% P.A. of Rs 10000/- to buy these shares and you are going to receive an annual dividend of 200% on a share of ABC Pvt. ltd having a face value of Rs1. Thus, you are gaining Rs2 Per share in a year amounting to a total gain of Rs200 as dividend in a year.

200 is 2% of your total investment of Rs 10000/-

Thus, your cost of carry will be 6% (Interest Paid) -2% (Dividend Received) = 4%.

This indicates that your break-even price per share will be Rs104/-

Option

An option contract gives the buyer the right but no obligation to settle the contract at a pre-agreed rate on a given date in the future.

As Option removes the obligation part of forward or futures contract, it becomes costlier in comparison to forward and future and attracts a premium.

There are four types of options
Buy Call Right to buy & No obligation to buy
Sell Call Obligation to Sell
Buy Put Right to sell but no obligation to sell
Sell Put Obligation to buy

A call option gives the buyer the right to buy the underlying on a given date in the future at a pre-agreed price but the buyer will not be under any obligation to buy the underlying if the price moves against him.

Let's, understand it by an example;

XYZ has entered an option contract with you on 15th November 2021 to buy 100 shares of Amazon at a rate of $3700 per share on 30th of November 2021.

On 30th November 2021, the scenario could be

Party	No of Shares	Market Price	Agreement Price	P&L
Buy Call (XYZ)	100(B)	3600	3700	XYZ will buy from the market @ $3600 and ignore the option contract.
Sell call (You)	100(S)	3600	3700	Seller will gain premium received while selling the option as the buyer's buy call remain unexercised.
Buy call (XYZ)	100 (B)	3800	3700	XYZ will buy from you @ $3700 / share
Sell call (You)	100 (S)	3800	3700	You are under obligation to sell 100 shares to XYZ @ $3700 per share even when the market price is 3800

Now the question arises why somcone will sell an option when there is such a huge risk?

The most probable reason could be that he is expecting the share prices to remain range-bound or to move in his favour so that he can gain profit from the premium received from the buyer of the option.

When the share prices move against the seller's position by price higher than the premium received by the seller the loss will start accumulating for the seller of the option.

Fundamental Analysis

The market reacts differently to different factors. Some of the key factors impacting market movements are Inflation, Gross Domestic Product, Interest Rates, Industrial Production, Socio-economic scenario, Geopolitical issues, etc.

We have already discussed Inflation and its impact on the economy & stock prices previously so will avoid repetition and will discuss other important factors in this part.

GDP

Gross domestic product is an indicator of the performance of an economy. It indicates how the growth drivers of an economy are performing. GDP growth is shown in comparison to a base year. In general, an increase in GDP indicates overall positive sentiments towards an economy and results in appreciation of the share prices.

Interest rates & liquidity position

Interest rates play an important role in the availability of overall liquidity in the system. A rise in interest rate by the central bank will suck liquidity from the system adversely impacting share prices.

In case of an increase in interest rates, investors will be able to fetch higher returns by keeping their surplus in banks at minimum risk. This discourages investors to invest money in the stock market where the risk is relatively higher.

Bank's also park their surplus money with the central bank to fetch safe returns instead of venturing into risky segments like stock markets.

Central bank reduces rates, generally to provide cheap fund to the economic growth instruments through banks. This fuels demand and thus drives industrial growth and also the expectation of investors for a better profitability of the companies. In such a scenario, stock prices generally move up as sentiments and expectations have turned positive further cheap money is now available for finding its way to the stock market.

Along with GDP & Inflation, some other key economic data impacting the market world across are;

Central Bank's Interest rate decisions

A rise in interest rate happens generally to tame increasing inflation. This will reduce liquidity from the system as investors will get higher returns by investing in relatively safer debt instruments than by investing in equities. A continuous increase in interest rates will hurt industrial activities. Companies will find difficulty in servicing interests on borrowed money and thus will avoid taking fresh loans for expansion, impacting their growth prospects and hitting their investor's expectations.

The emerging economies are getting huge foreign investments because of higher interest rate differentials as well as better return prospects. But if the interest rates start increasing in developed economies like the US, Europe then investors from these countries will find it better to invest in their economies rather than to venture into other emerging economies and take an additional r by way of currency exchange risk.

This interest rate differential between two economies is a key driver of the movement of funds from one country to another and ultimately one of the key reasons for the direction of stock markets of a particular economy.

Industrial Production of major economies

Industrial production data indicates the industrial activity happening in a particular country. Higher industrial production figures indicate better activity and bright prospects for the economic growth of the given country and thus higher stock prices of companies in the given economy.

US Non-Farm Payroll

US is a major player in world financial markets and anything happening in the US will certainly have an impact on the markets across the world. An increase in non-farm payrolls indicates better industrial activities in the US. This indicates positive sentiments towards the economy and encourages investors to invest in risky assets.

Quarterly financial results of listed companies

Besides the general economic and political scenarios, one factor which impacts a stock in any situation is the company's performance.

An intelligent investor, tracks the company's financial performances, future plans, management capabilities and if these are indicating negative or relatively lower performance, then the investor will quickly switch to other stock with a better perspective for growth.

Change in Key Management

The market generally reacts to corporate actions. A sudden exit by key management personnel is taken as negative when general stock sentiments are positive. Management is responsible for driving the company in the right direction and if key management personnel is leaving then the market takes it as a caution.

Credit rating agencies

Credit rating agencies are now a days playing a big role. Market players are watching every movement of credit rating agencies and treat their announcements as signals. A rating downgrade of a country or company is treated as negative and investors move away from such stocks/ markets.

For foreign investment funds, the rating is a key benchmark they have to follow and as per the given mandate, they can invest only in securities/markets with a rating above their benchmarked rating.

As soon as the rating of such stock/market deteriorates and goes below the minimum threshold, the investment fund is bound by the mandates given by its investors to exit such positions/markets.

Geo-political scenario

History has shown us that with slight negative news of any escalation in the geopolitical scenario, the stock prices of relevant countries tumble down quickly. It's better to keep away from the market in such uncertain scenarios to play safe but at the same time do not lose focus as such scenarios are the ones when you will get an opportunity to buy value stock of fundamentally strong companies at cheaper rates.

In all such negative scenarios and when the market has corrected substantially, an intelligent investor can pick fundamentally strong companies' stocks through SIP mode. SIP mode brings down the average price in a falling market.

I f you look at historical patterns in equity indices, it can be easily observed that when the markets were significantly down due to some negative news, those were the best times to invest in the market for making sizable returns.

For a value investor, this is the best time to pick quality stocks available at beaten-down prices. With the first ray of hope emerging from the dark negative scenario, the markets quickly bounce back and most of the time bounce back much above the previous highs.

It can be seen from the above graph of Nifty, that the best returns were generated immediately after a significant crash.

Risk Mitigation

Investment in stock/equity is a relatively risky investment. An intelligent investor uses various tools to reduce this risk. Some of the key risk mitigators are;

Risk Management Policy

RMP is a document incorporating do's and don'ts to avoid taking excessive risk and the ways to mitigate risk. It can cover, the instruments company is permitted to use for risk mitigation, internal control, etc.

Stop Loss

An investor should have some level in his mind at which he should exit the position by booking a loss. Its human psychology to book profit immediately even when the stock has the potential to move further up but keep accumulating losses.

We don't want to lose but by not exiting the position we are losing principal amount and thus impacting our capacity to generate returns in the future as well. Let's understand it by an example

Shwan has invested $1000 out of the total investable corpus of $1500 in stock of ABC corporation ltd. at a share price of $10 per share. He was expecting a 20% profit in 6 months. He has a total holding of 100 shares.

The share price of ABC Corp has started falling and now reached $8 per share. Shawn does not want to book losses and thus continue with his investment even after losing 20% of his investment.

Now the investment amount reduced from $1000 to $800. To generate 20% returns over an initial investment of $1000, now the portfolio has to generate a return of $400/$800 i.e., 50%!!

An intelligent investor never fears booking losses. We have to go with the flow and should stop the temptation to outsmart the market. If a share is falling, it's better to exit at the pre-decided stop loss level than to lose the entire principal amount.

All Eggs in One Basket

This is another mistake investors do. Investing total investable amount only in one or two stock might give good returns but there is a risk that it can result in heavy losses if these chosen stock does not perform.

For sustainable growth, investors should create a portfolio of stocks. In a portfolio, some stocks will generate losses while some will generate profit. What matters is the overall profit generation and reduction in losses.

It is not necessary to have plenty of stocks in your portfolio. A thoroughly studied portfolio of even 5-10 stocks can generate better returns.

Diversification is a key step in risk mitigation be it stock market trading or some other business. Even for a common man, diversification of his investments is a key risk mitigation strategy.

Value investing

Value investing is a very useful risk mitigating strategy. An intelligent investor invests in a fundamentally strong company that is available at a good discount. This reduces the chance of incurring significant losses, as the stock has already corrected significantly in comparison to the fundamental position of the company but at the same time increases the probability of generating higher returns over time.

The knee-jerk reaction of markets to news does not impact the performance of strong companies over time and thus an intelligent investor should use this opportunity to accumulate a stock of such a fundamentally strong company that is available at great discounts. The markets will most likely realign after some time with the fundamentals.

Active vs passive investment

Active investment means an investor is keen to earn market-beating returns and thus looks for opportunities in the market to realign his portfolio at quick intervals. As against active investment, passive investment generally means framing a policy and then investing for the long term based on a predefined investment policy. The passive investor generally invests in funds tracking some benchmark like NIFTY, GOLD, etc.

There is no guarantee that active investment can generate returns better than passive investment.

In fact, in the case of active investment, the investor is paying more to the broker on account of the churning of the portfolio.

Further active investment requires more time of the investor. He needs to track the market, identify the stocks, and then watch the news for shifting portfolio but in passive investment, all these works are delegated to the mutual fund tracking the desired benchmark.

For a novice investor, passive investment through a mutual fund is advisable in comparison to getting involved in identifying the stocks and then tracking them as is required under active fund management, let the professional fund managers do it for them through mutual funds.

VIX: An Opportunity or Risk

Volatility is the rate and magnitude of change in price & Volatility index is a measure of the market's expectation of volatility over the near term. Volatility is treated as risk, the returns on a portfolio can vary significantly in a volatile phase.

The volatility index is a measure, of the amount by which the underlying index is expected to fluctuate in the near term.

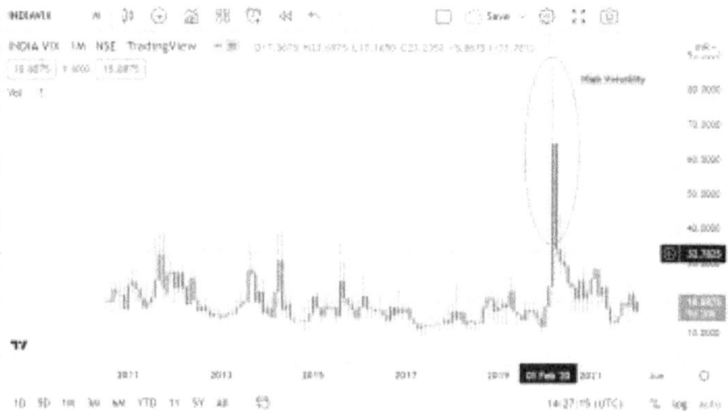

The above graph represents the volatility in the Indian stock market. This shows extreme spikes in between dull periods. An investor can take a call to be in the market or to exit by tracking this graph.

In short, this volatility index is also termed as India VIX. It indicates the degree of fluctuation traders are expecting over the next 30 days in the Nifty 50 Index.

India VIX was introduced by the NSE in 2008, but the concept was originally introduced by Chicago Board Options Exchange in 1993.

The value for India VIX is derived by using the Black & Scholes (B&S) Model.

The India VIX uses five variables – strike price, the market price of a stock, time to expiry, the risk-free rate, and volatility. The VIX arrives at the volatility expected by the traders in the market by using the best bid and ask quotes of the out-of-the-money, present, and near-month Nifty option contracts.

A higher value of India VIX indicates higher volatility expectations in the Nifty and a lower value of India VIX indicates lower volatility expectations.

Assume the India VIX value is 18. This means that the traders expect 18 percent volatility for the next 30 days. In other words, traders expect the value of the Nifty to be in a range between +18 percent and -18 percent from the current Nifty value for the next year over the next 30 days.

Theoretically, VIX ranges between 15 and 35. Anything around or below 15 would suggest low volatility but if it is above 35, we can say volatility is high.

Historically India VIX has a strong negative correlation with Nifty. When the India VIX falls, the Nifty is seen to rising and vice versa.

Financial Ratios

Price to Earnings Ratio

The price to earnings ratio (P/E) is the ratio of a company's share price to the company's earnings per share (EPS). It is an indicator to know how expensive a stock is in comparison to other stocks of the same industry. P/E ratio can also be used to ascertain how the overall benchmark is performing in comparison to the earnings of the corporations which are part of this benchmark.

Price-earnings ratio (PE ratio) is the monetary value that a market participant is willing to pay for every rupee of earnings of a company.

Index P/E can be arrived at by dividing Index Market Capitalization by Gross Earning

Index P/E= Index Market Capitalization / Gross Earnings

Index market capitalization = (Total of the outstanding equity shares or units considered for index computation) x (closing price of each index constituent adjusted for factors such as free-float, capping factor, etc).

Earnings= The earnings reported by each index constituent in the trailing 4 quarters are accumulated and adjusted for factors such as free-float, capping factor, etc.

(Source: nseindia.com)

P/E ratio is traditionally used to ascertain how much overvalued or undervalued the current market or a particular stock is trading in comparison to its past trend. For example, NIFTY 50 which is trading on the date of writing this book i.e., April 2021 at 33.60 against a high of 40.80 in Feb 2021. Normally the average PE ratio for NIFTY 50 is around 19-26. This indicates that even after falling from 40.80 PE to 33.60 PE, the market is still overvalued and trading at a much higher PE than its general average.

For a medium-long term investor, tracking the PE ratio is very useful. When the PE ratio of the broader market is near to its lower band, that is the right time to enter into the market & when it is near to its higher end of the band, that is the time to exit the market. Further, if the investor is not certain about which stock to choose, he can simply go by portfolio allocation in line with the constituents of the benchmark in a similar proportion as the individual share contributes to the benchmark. It is a passive investment strategy as the result generated will be more or less similar to the return generated by the index with some difference on account of tracking error.

You can find historical nifty PE ratios at **https://www1.nseindia.com/products/content/equities/indices/historical_pepb.htm**

Earnings per share

Earnings per share is one of the key financial indicators used by fundamental investors in finding stocks for value investing.

Basic EPS and diluted EPS are used to measure the profitability of a company.

Basic EPS

Basic EPS takes into account the company's outstanding common equity shares while diluted EPS includes employee stock options, warrants, convertible debts (bonds) which can be converted to equity or common stocks.

In the case of convertible securities, new shares are issued, thus the number of shares increases, resulting in a reduction of EPS.

As the number of shares is increasing on account of the inclusion of convertible stocks, the dilution of EPS takes place and thus it's called diluted EPS.

It measures the earnings of the company on a per-share basis.

This can be a very useful metric to compare different companies' performances from the investor's point of view.

$$EPS = \frac{\text{Net Income} - \text{Preferred Stock Dividends}}{\text{Average Outstanding Shares}}$$

Preferred stock dividends are dividends that though are not guaranteed but get priority over common stock dividends.

	No of Shares O/S (in cr.)	Net Income (in crore)	Basic EPS
FY 2020	359.74	-12070	-33.55
FY 2019	339.58	-18826	-84.88

In this case, as the company is loss-making, thus EPS is negative. An investor generally looks for higher EPS.

In the case of the early stages of a company the income will be low, in such cases, the EPS will be either very low or negative. An investor needs to look beyond EPS to understand the value in the company to take an investment decision.

Diluted EPS

In the case of diluted EPS, it is assumed that all convertible securities are converted to equity i.e., the right by the security holder to convert the securities to equity is exercised.

$$\text{Diluted EPS} = \frac{\text{Net Income} - \text{Preferred Stock Dividends}}{\text{Average Out. Shares} + \text{dilutive Shares}}$$

Diluted EPS can also be treated as a worst-case scenario when all the convertible securities are converted to equity thus impacting the earning per share of the company.

As in the case of diluted EPS, the denominator is increasing without having any impact on the numerator, thus the diluted EPS will be lower than basic EPS in cases where the company has convertible securities, else the diluted EPS will be equal to basic EPS.

Cash EPS

For working cash EPS, non-cash expenses like depreciation are added back to the net profit & loss to arrive at net income. It is the operating cash flow of the company divided by the number of out-standing shares.

$$\text{Cash EPS} = \frac{\text{Operating Cash Flow}}{\text{Diluted Outstanding Shares}}$$

	No of Shares O/S (in cr.)	Net Income + Depreciation (in cr.)	Cash EPS
FY 2020	359.74	10450	29.04
FY 2019	339.58	-5343	-15.73

A company with higher cash EPS is assumed to have better capability to generate cash flow and thus better financial performance.

Cash EPS is less prone to accounting manipulation and thus is a useful tool for comparison.

Now the question arises, which EPS is good?

The answer to this question is, each EPS serves its purpose and a user of the balance sheet needs to take care to use similar metrics to compare the financial performance of different companies or a company's historic performance.

Book Value

Book value is the net assets value of a firm. The equation for arriving book value is

Book Value = Total Assets – Total Liabilities

We also know that Total assets- Total Liabilities = Net Worth

Thus, we can assume that

Book value = Net Worth

Net worth = Shareholder's equity + Retained Earnings

This is the amount that investors are entitled to get in case of liquidation of a company after meeting its liabilities.

The book value of an asset is the original purchase price of the asset – accumulated depreciation.

Book value per share

Book value per share is calculated by subtracting all debt, liabilities, and the liquidation price of preferred stock from the company's total assets and then dividing the value arrived by the number of outstanding shares of common stock.

$$BVPS = \frac{\text{Total Shareholder's equity – preferred equity}}{\text{Total outstanding common shares}}$$

Value investor will always look for shares of company's trading near to their book values or below their book value. The more the share price of a company is trading close to or below the book value, the greater will be the safety of principal (subject to other fundamental aspects).

Legendary investors like Benjamin Graham, Warren Buffett have used this as a key part of their investment strategy to build fortunes.

Inflated assets will inflate the net worth, which in turn inflate the book value per share. Thus, it makes the job of a prudent investor more difficult.

An investor should not be guided only by the balance sheet figures of shareholders' equity value but also use the accounting concepts as advised in International Accounting Standards to ascertain the correctness in the classification of assets and liabilities in the balance sheet.

Particularly in the case of unlisted companies, it becomes challenging to find the exact book value per share.

When book value per share exceeds the market value of the share, the stock is deemed as undervalued.

The book value per share can be increased by either reducing the average outstanding common stocks or by increasing net assets.

Companies repurchase their stocks to reduce the average outstanding shares and thus improve the book value per share.

The second way is by keeping the liabilities at the lower side and increasing the net assets, thus increasing the net worth.

In the case of asset light companies like software companies which generally have a very low value of assets, the book value will be very low. Thus, comparing book values of companies in the different sectors will not give proper results and thus an investor should compare book values of companies in a similar sector only.

Before using book value to use as a tool for investment, an investor should also ascertain reasons for the company's stock trading below its book value. The probable reason could be

- Lack of investor's confidence
- Fundamentally weak company
- Loss-making company
- Inflated net worth by use of creative accounting.

A company will have negative book value when, the company has higher liabilities in comparison to assets, thus indicating financial weakness and balance sheet insolvency.

	Shareholders' Equity	Shares O/S	BVPS
FY 2020	63078	359.74	175.34
FY 2019	60179	339.58	177.21

Price to Book Ratio

The price to book ratio is used to compare companies' market capitalization to its book value thus, reflecting the company's net assets available to common shareholders relative to the market price of its stock.

$$\text{P/B Ratio} = \frac{\text{Market Price Per Share}}{\text{Book Value Per Share}}$$

A ratio higher than one, indicates the market is willing to pay a higher price for the company's shares than its net asset price.

A company with less than one P/B ratio indicates investors are unwilling to pay a price higher than the book price. The reason could be a lack of confidence by investors in the fundamental growth prospects of the company.

A high-growth company will generally have a P/B ratio way above one while a financially distressed company will generally have a P/B ratio below one.

The interpretation of a lower P/B ratio by a value investor can be different. A company with a lower P/B value ratio is an opportunity subject to the fundamental position & growth prospects of the company are strong.

A value investor will look for a fundamentally strong company with a P/B ratio less than one or lower than the industry average.

An investor should not discard a company if its P/B ratio is less than one, he should go deep into the company's financials, its management, its growth prospects, industry scenario, record, news related to the company and then only should decide on whether to invest or leave the stock.

The market value of a share is generally higher than the book value and thus it's an opportunity if the investor is getting a share of a fundamentally strong company at the book value or lower than the book value.

The basic difference between Market Value and Book Value is market value is the forward-looking value of a company's equity and thus reflects the company's growth prospects while book value is based on historic data.

There is no specific P/B ratio that can be treated as good or bad, an investor needs to compare the industry ratio with the company's ratio to ascertain if the share is available at a decent price or not.

A good P/B ratio for one industry can be bad for another industry, thus comparing companies in a similar sector is important.

Return on Equity

Return on equity is a tool in fundamental analysis of balance sheet and used to find out the percentage of return generated by a company over its equity. It is used to compare companies in a similar industry and to find out companies generating better returns on equity. Companies generating a higher return on equity can be attractive for investors.

$$ROE = \frac{\text{Net Income}}{\text{Average shareholder's equity}}$$

Net income is the income after netting off expenses and taxes paid during a given period.

Further, for calculating ROE the net income is arrived at after dividends paid to preferred shareholders & interest paid to lenders but before allocation of dividends to common shareholders.

ROE is a useful tool in evaluating investment returns. An investor can compare the industry average ROE with the company's ROE to form a view on the profit-generating capability of the targeted company.

A company with ROE higher than the industry average or peer group will be the preferred company for investors. ROE gives an insight into the effective use of shareholders' capital for generating returns by the company's management.

An investor needs to ascertain the historical trend in ROE. A sustainable and increasing ROE over time indicates the company to be a worthy investment option.

While an irregular and decreasing ROE indicates financial troubles and investors generally do not give such company preference over other steady ROE generating company because a decreasing ROE indicates that management is not able to use investor money properly or are using money in non-productive assets.

A user of a balance sheet needs to be careful in taking a decision based on ROE. A very high ROE can be on account of very low shareholder equity. It indicates that the promoter's stake is very low in a company and thus the company can be prone to risk as promoters will lose interest as soon as the company lends in some financial trouble because promoters don't have much at risk.

Further, it can also indicate that the company is using very high debt in comparison to equity to fund its business, resulting in higher leverage. Very high leverage is generally negative for an investor.

Similarly, a company in the initial period of operations or project under implementation can have very low ROE as the returns generated will be small in comparison to the equity investment.

Another case for very high ROE could be a company incurring loss in the previous year thus eroding its capital and then a sudden profit on account of higher business, accounting change or tax returns, etc can inflate the ratio as the denominator has reduced.

To overcome this, investors need to compare past trends, industry averages, or peer group averages.

Further investor also needs to take care that the company is in profit and its net shareholder's equity is also positive because a negative income and negative shareholder equity can also give positive ROE.

The multiplying effect of leverage on ROE can be understood by the following equation

$$ROE = \frac{Net\ Income}{Total\ Asset} \times \frac{Total\ Assets}{Equity}$$

$$ROE = ROA \times Leverage$$

Dividend Payout Ratio

The dividend payout ratio is the ratio of dividends paid out to the shareholders out of the total net income of the company. The dividend is paid out of profits and if a company is in loss, then the question of payment of the dividend does not arise.

Companies are not under compulsion to pay a dividend; they can retain a part or full profit for future expansion of business and growth.

Many investors invest in stocks of companies having a history of paying consistent dividends. Apart from the increase in the share price of a stock on account of higher public interest, the dividend adds up to the gains for the shareholders.

The dividend paid also compensates to a certain extent for the fall in prices of stocks.

An investor expects companies not paying a dividend and retaining profits to generate a higher return by way of an increase in share price.

A conservative prudent investor will prefer stocks with consistent dividend payout history over other stocks. An investor has to find a balance between dividend-paying stocks and growth stocks.

Growth stocks are generally stocks of companies that are in the growth stage and thus use the retained profits for subsequent growth of the company, thus not paying a dividend or paying divided at a low rate.

But the stock price of such companies generally rises much faster and thus compensating the loss on account of non-payment of dividends.

Regular payment of dividend indicates ethical management practice as dividend is a right of shareholder. A shareholder has invested in the company to receive dividend and if a company persistently choose not to pay dividend, then it is not doing justice with the shareholder's rights.

The dividend payout ratio indicates, how much the company is paying to its shareholders and how much it is retaining for future growth, debt payment, etc.

$$\text{Dividend Payout Ratio} = \frac{\text{Dividend Paid}}{\text{Net Income}}$$

Retention Ratio = 1- Dividend Payout Ratio

It can also be defined in terms of the per-share ratio

$$\text{Retention Ratio} = \frac{\text{EPS-DPS}}{\text{EPS}}$$

EPS = Earnings per share & DPS = Dividend per share

The dividend payout ratio is also industry-specific and a user of the balance sheet should compare companies in a similar sector only for better comparison.

Real Estate Investment Trust or Infrastructure Investment Trust are under obligation to distribute 90% of the profit generated in a given financial year as dividends thus cannot be compared with other sectors.

A very high dividend payout can also be negative for the investor. It might indicate that the company is hiding something from the investor and to divert their attention to paying higher dividends.

It can also indicate that the company is not focusing on future growth and not investing the profit generated for further improvement of the business. Thus, there has to be a fine balance between retention and dividend payment.

An investor should look for regular dividend-paying companies. Consistency is more important than a one-off large dividend payment.

For comparing companies having different share prices, dividend yield can be a better metric.

$$\text{Dividend Yield} = \frac{\text{Dividend per share}}{\text{Price per share}}$$

Margin of Safety

Margin of safety is a concept in which investors invest in stocks only when they are available at a significant discount to its intrinsic value. The thought is that downside risk will be lower in such stocks and the upside potential is higher.

Margin of safety does not guarantee good returns or protection against loss of principal but if done along with fundamental analysis can to a greater extent reduce the chances of incurring significant losses.

For finding a stock with a higher margin of safety, an investor should be in a position to work out the intrinsic value of the stock. For calculating intrinsic value, a formula is given by **Benjamin Graham** in his book The **Intelligent Investor** (a must-read)

Intrinsic value = Earnings per share ×

[(8.5 + (2 × Expected annual growth rate, g)]

EPS is the last 12-month trailing earnings per share

8.5 is taken as P/E base for no growth company

The expected growth rate is the estimated growth rate over 7 to 10 years.

The above formula is revised in 1974, in the revised edition of The Intelligent Investor;

Intrinsic value = [EPS × (8.5 + 2g) × 4.4]/Y

In this formula, 4.4 is the then prevailing (1962) rate on high-grade corporate bonds listed on the New York Stock Exchange. Y is the current yield on AAA-rated corporate bonds.

For an investor, who is not very comfortable in using the formulas, he can simply watch for stocks that have fallen significantly but are fundamentally strong and are falling because of some temporary event. These can be a good target for value investing. But be careful in understanding the reason for such a fall and should invest in the company only if the fall is not attributed to fundamental weakness.

In such cases systematic purchase can be a good option as no one knows to which level the stock will fall, thus purchasing through a SIP will reduce the risk and give an average price for the investment.

Also, an investor needs to have the patience to resist jumping to take a position when a stock is falling and should understand the causes of such a fall.

If the broader market is falling then any stock will fall but that allows valuing investors to accumulate quality stocks at attractive prices.

Further, watch out for stocks that are fundamentally strong but are trading below the average price of their peer group of stocks. For this, an investor can use the P/E ratio, P/B ratio, etc.

In any case, a value investor should shy away from stocks that are fundamentally weak or are overvalued as the margin for safety will generally be very low.

About the author

Raj Kumar Sharma, a banker by profession and writer by choice, has experience in different segments of banking and finance. Grown-up in a modest town of central India, Bhopal, Raj Kumar has completed his graduation from Bhopal University.

He got the inspiration to write books during his stint as a trainer in one of the prestigious training institutes of a leading bank in India. The Eureka moment came when his work got recognition in competitions organized by the National Institute of Bank Management-Pune & Indian Institute of Banking & Finance. He likes to write on both fiction and non-fiction topics.

Other books by the author

Ratio Analysis

Ratio Analysis is an integral part of the assessment of the financial position of an organization. By analyzing ratios one can get a fair idea of the health of the organization. Ratio analysis gives an insight into the operational efficiency, liquidity, leverage, solvency & profitability of the organization.

This book briefs about the key financial ratios & their importance in decision-making. These ratios are important not only in providing any debt support to the company but also in deciding to invest in the shares of the company. For any investor who wishes to learn fundamental analysis of stocks, this book is a first step towards the same.

Balance Sheet Analysis

Anyone who wishes to have a career in a bank or any financial segment including stock broking /investing, it becomes important for him to be well versed with a basic understanding of the balance sheet. This book is an effort by the author to explain terms used in the balance sheet in a very user-friendly language. It is a must-read for fundamental investors / new bankers.

Export Business- A Beginner's Guide

Many of us have somewhere deep in our hearts a wish to become an entrepreneur. Due to the unavailability of the right information, many of us were unable to venture into this promising segment of international trade and remained confined to meeting our day-to-day needs.

This book is an attempt to bring the much-needed information in one place to enable a prospective entrepreneur to venture into international trade. This book tries to bridge the crucial knowledge gap and provide information on areas related to international trade.

This book enables the prospective entrepreneurs to have a know-how of legal requirements, the way to find markets & buyers, the requirement of different countries, the risk involved, the risk mitigation measures, the documentation, and the process involved.

My Choice My Life

This book is based on small day-to-day events which occur in a common human being's life and how we can learn from these incidences to re-shape our way of conducting ourselves and to improve upon. In any situation, we will have more than one way to react to the situation and if we give ourselves a little time then we can realize immediately which way is the right one.

Destination-Beyond Frontiers

A science fiction novel taking its readers on an adventurous journey into the unknown space. A work of fiction inspired by discoveries and inventions by humans.

Declaration

Contents of this book have nothing to do with the organization author works for and views and ideas expressed in the book were the author's personal view.

www.ingramcontent.com/pod-product-compliance
Lightning Source LLC
Chambersburg PA
CBHW050336160726
48002CB00001B/339